W9-DDC-956

BEYOND PEARL HARBOR

BEYOND PEA

RL HARBOR

by James J. Martin

PLOWSHARE PRESS Little Current, Ontario

BEYOND PEARL HARBOR   ISBN #0-919077-02-1

PLOWSHARE PRESS   RR1, Little Current,
Ontario POP 1KO, Canada

© 1981 by JAMES J. MARTIN   *All Rights Reserved*

Designed by *George Yamada*

"Pearl Harbor, Antecedents, Background and Consequences" and "The Framing of 'Tokyo Rose' " were first published in *The Saga of Hog Island*, 1977, reprinted by permission of Ralph Myles, Publisher, Inc., P. O. Box 1533, Colorado Springs, Colorado 80901.

The review of *Years of Infamy* by Michi Weglyn is reprinted from *Libertarian Review*, November 1978 by permission of Libertarian Review, Inc., San Francisco, California 94111.

Previously unpublished material incorporated in this edition copyright by James J. Martin, May 1981.

To the Memory of

YONÉ

Who Understood What It Cost
To Fight the Good Fight

Contents

Introduction

THROUGHOUT history there are spectacular and singular happenings of such dramatic circumstances that they seem to hang suspended in time, all other actions and proceedings halted at those moments as though frozen. In our recent past, two such events in particular seem to qualify for inclusion in such a category: the attack on Pearl Harbor of December 7, 1941 and the atomic bombing of Hiroshima on August 6, 1945. One imagines these stunning occurrences as almost pendant backdrops to subsequent events as though incapable of being dispersed. Every time we once more see moving pictures of them we can imagine easily that the billowing smoke and the explosions at Pearl Harbor actually are still being experienced there, as we also can imagine the stupefying mushroom cloud and unbelievable dazzling light of the atomic shot over Hiroshima nearly four years later.

Journalism and pictured entertainment are heavily responsible for this illusion, as well as for draining them of relationship of all kinds, especially political, as though they were simply staged spectacles, following which the props were dismantled and carried off to be restructured for still another somewhere else to make us gasp in amazement and almost dazed prostration. Few are impressed with their consequences, and even fewer are made aware of their origins. It is easier by far to believe that such incredible affairs are indeed tableaux of massive design with intended assault on the senses so vast that there really is no reason for carrying any further rumination or speculation as to their real place in the history of our days. It is in this sense that the title of this brief collection of essays bears the word "Beyond" within it. In actuality there is no intent to work them into the fabric of world politics for the last 40 years, nor to make the collection an exhaustive survey of all the massive changes that have followed, especially in East Asia, since the end of the Pacific War. The emphasis has been on a select few events preceding that conflict as well as unseen consequences growing from unanticipated forces and conditions this war unleashed, the stress being on the happenstance and fortuitous rather than the expectable, the predictable or the logical. It is the purpose of this introduction to deal with many aspects which belong under these latter headings.

Among those for whom the Pearl Harbor drama is not already as remote as Roncesvalles, research continues and revelations are noted, genially ignored by the producers of pious puffs upholding the old fairy tales, as though everything had already been placed on the record by the circle and the elements with a vital stake in the preservation of Establishment veracity. Its fundamental plea is the claim of utter, total innocence of an impending attack upon American installations and fleet in Hawaii. Its attending corollaries are (1) complete ignoring of the nature of politics and war in Asia at the time in 1941, as though the Pearl Harbor affair was simply a mindless and isolated stunt, and (2) a similar blackout of the domestic scene in the weeks and then days prior to the attack, as though public communications lacked even the tiniest smidgin of attention to the likely consequences of the crisis of the fall of 1941. Two essays in this brief collection deal with Pearl Harbor, and pay attention to new information surfacing in the last dozen or so years, but it might be mentioned that a respectable compendium of material, including accounts which actually picked Pearl Harbor as the site of the coming attack weeks before it happened, could be collected from American newspapers and magazines widely circulated late in 1941. These alone indicate that the wail of innocence and outrage which promptly rose to the heavens on December 7, 1941 was spurious and misplaced.

Time magazine, with its immense readership, in its lamentably-timed issue (December 8), gloated about the vast American and British war machine which was allegedly ready to spring on the Japanese, should they snap under President Franklin D. Roosevelt's "war of nerves" and "undeclared war," and react militarily. And Hallett Abend, a widely-read newspaper reporter on matters Japanese in those days, in his November 18, 1941 *Look* magazine article, "How the U.S. Navy Will Fight Japan," which was exposed to a potential readership of about 12,000,000 Americans, included the following delicious morsel:

> When the clash comes, the Japanese fleet will have to stay in home waters, to guard the islands of the [Japanese] Empire, against [U.S.] naval raids. Our own fleet will cruise somewhere west of Hawaii, with scout planes far over the sea day and night to prevent surprise raids on the Pearl Harbor naval base or on our own West Coast cities.

The State Department, the War Department, and the Army Chief of Staff, the latter two responsible for the defense of both the base at Honolulu and the fleet when it was in the harbor, apparently were not among Abend's readers. But a veritable wheel barrow full of similar journalism could easily be assembled, and those who were reading Abend and others writing in the above vein should not have affected a pose of surprise and shock over the events of that fateful Sunday 40 years ago. After all, *Time*, in its issue referred to above, had comfortingly assured all that "Everyone was ready from Rangoon to Honolulu, every man was at battle stations." In view of this mass of contemporary literature of wide circulation expecting war at any time in those tense days, one may be led to wonder how the legend of treacherous "surprise attack" ever got off the ground.

But the response even now reflects a general viewpoint in harmony with the belief that we are dealing in the main with an isolated occurrence unrelated to Asian history or world affairs, and to be considered even now as a subjective event to be seen through the eyes of a politically ignorant sailor several decks down on an exploding ship or a housewife standing on a rooftop five miles from the embattled Base, describing the smoke and the noise of the explosions. And the editorial writers still produce copy which reads like contemporary indignant screeds. The gout of self-serving evasive and irrelevant wrath which boiled forth on the 40th anniversary of the Pearl Harbor bombing in the U.S. press was a remarkable confirmation of the observation made nearly five centuries ago by the anonymous observer, in his four-word 'review' of Poggio Bracciolini's lopsided partisan history of Florence ("good patriot, bad historian"), on how easy it still is to be simultaneously such a proper patriot and execrable historian. For most journalists it was simply another occasion to tie the past into contemporary opportunism and to use it to buttress current policy in one way or another. So the usual two-level perception of reality continues, one prepared for the general public and quite another for the serious historical students. Essentially the former product comes under the heading of what George Orwell described as "prolefeed," casual diversionary trivia intended to mystify and mollify, while entertaining, the vast semi-informed populace. Little if any of the war that ensued is allowed to complicate the presented spectacle.

In the sense that modern war is first of all an industrial pitting of national production strengths the Pacific War represented two gigantic clusters of major industries in conflict. Nevertheless, the Japanese were wholly outclassed from the start in total size, capitalization, labor force, resources and general wherewithal. The remarkable thing is that the forces of Imperial Japan persisted so long. Though in eventual total and profound defeat, their overall performance was not lost on East Asians, and its impressiveness may never be forgotten by them, whatever devices may have been employed by their conquerors to make its conduct appear 'immoral' and reprehensible (this maneuver has been employed against the vanquished since antiquity.)

The collapse of Euro-American colonialism, despite the 'victory,' was swift and drastic. Since its preservation was a major factor in American policy leading to the confrontation, we may begin here by noting a spectacular demise of a major war aim of the 'victorious.' The subsequent incredible industrial expansion of all the Far East and all the attendant changes of the last 30 years are integrally related to the course and outcome of that war. Japanese resurgence and their remarkable pressure in the industrial and commercial world today remind one of Lawrence Dennis' reflection on the "bloody futility of frustrating the strong." One may observe here that all this has seemingly taken place without any expenditure of blood at all. But the breaking of the impasse and logjam of the 1930s in the Pacific War was its presaging. Surely things could not have gone on that way very much longer; the war of 1941-45 simply detoured the course of events a few years.

There is little need to dwell upon 'misunderstanding' and 'lack of communication' as war causes, though these surely were abominably bad, no matter what angle one wants to pursue. Japan had a considerable exposure in the American press, almost all invidious, whether it emanated from patrician Ivy League Japanophobe political adversaries such as Henry L. Stimson, or from the Stalinist, Trotzkyite and pro-Maoist columnists and reporters who proliferated in the papers and magazines, and political advisers of similar stripe who flourished behind the scenes. The latter seemed to be concerned more about future Chinese than Japanese affairs, but surely recognized that a Red China was out of the question until the Japanese had been driven from mainland Asia. So came years of malicious misrepresentation convincing Americans that the Japanese were utterly beyond the pale of respectability for their alleged limitless 'militarism.'

How tiny the funnel was through which actual Japanese information got to Americans was revealed after war was under way. Archibald MacLeish, Librarian of Congress and one of the Roosevelt regime's principal propaganda chiefs, asserted that there were in his opinion only *three* non-Japanese in the entire U.S.A. at Pearl Harbor time with a real command of Japanese language. *Publishers Weekly* (September 26, 1942, p. 1192) suggested this was too small, and believed the number to be one hundred. But even this is a microscopically small percentage of a country then of about 132,000.000. Unique among commentaries on Japan and its people was John Patric's *Yankee Hobo in the Orient,* issued originally by Doubleday early in 1945 before the war was over as *Why Japan Was Strong,* and which by the end of the 1940s must have been read in its many translations around the world by 12,000,000 persons. Its sympathetic and understanding portrait of the Japanese people must have shocked many Americans, though overstated was his conclusion that most of what was wrong and undesirable about Japan was its Statism. Surely their version was an extremely muted form when compared with that of the U.S.A.'s noble 'ally,' Soviet Russia, accentuated undoubtedly by the aggravated poverty of the 1930s decade, when Patric wandered about Japan almost at will. Material such as this, had it been widespread here in the decade before the war came about, might have had some modifying effect. (An absorbing summary of American misconceptions about the Japanese in the period ending about March, 1941 can be found in Porter Sargent's *Getting US Into War* (Boston, 1941), "Prodding Japan Into War," pp. 525-545.)

But communication was not noticeably better on many other levels, including the diplomatic. Stimson, while Secretary of State under Pres. Herbert C. Hoover, during the crisis of 1931-32 involving Japan in Manchuria and North China, utilized a novel device to cut down on 'discourse' with the Japanese. According to the two anonymous journalists who wrote *High Low Washington* (Philadelphia: Lippincott, 1932, pp. 159-61), Stimson excluded all Japanese foreign correspondents from his press conferences in these times, presumably on the grounds that they lacked sufficient command of English to grasp the tortured writhings through which the Secretary of State sought to present American positions in his "agonizing acrobatics," as the authors, in attendance themselves, described the fumbling proceedings. (Stimson did far better later on as Roosevelt's Secretary of War and was much clearer as to what he 'meant' in 1940-1941, in particular.)

And under Roosevelt, and his Secretary of State, Cordell Hull, a few months later, the situation got no better, and, subsequently, much worse. The Japanese view that Japan was as entitled to a separate power position in Asia via a device approximating the Monroe Doctrine, behind which Roosevelt increasingly functioned in extending, ultimately, American power virtually to the western coast of Africa, was denounced in the pre-Pearl Harbor decade. The rigid unwillingness to recognize this obviously played a big part in bringing about war. Only now are we noticing attention to this matter which is sober and appreciative, not a distillation of snorts and catcalls, denunciation and ridicule. Some serious attention is due to the points made by Dr. Gerald K. Haines in his

v

"American Myopia and the Japanese Monroe Doctrine," published in the *Prologue Journal of the National Archives* (Summer, 1981, vol. 13, no. 2, pp. 101-114).

If the Pearl Harbor story is still conducted on two levels, depending on the intelligence, general knowledge, sophistication and experience of the audience aimed at, so are the other events of high drama, from the war itself all through to the atomic bombing conclusion, and including what passes for explanation of the world that has resulted to the present day. What did the U.S.A. go to war for, other than as retaliation for Pearl Harbor? Surely the American public would never have entered a war so enthusiastically and fought with such desperate devotion unless its aims had been lowered to a very primitive common denominator. Fighting for the preservation of European colonies, the "Open Door," and the promotion of an opaque and complicated China policy never would have survived as projected goals. But fighting to exterminate the Japanese for their effrontery and obliterate their home islands, followed by a general incineration of East Asia if need be and a return home to peace and prosperity, seemed to prevail vaguely in many minds, and these bare and simple sentiments were not noticeably jogged by the war regime's propaganda. Japanophobia, cultivated by all means available, was so successful that it has not yet receded, despite tanks of ink and miles of film devoted to telling all that Japan is America's 'friend' now. Surely the decision to incarcerate *all* Japanese living on the U.S. mainland in concentration camps envisioned a goodly element of the wartime propaganda value accruing to such a program, and the decision to adopt such measures appears to be anything but a spinal cord reaction to the way things were going at the start of the war in December, 1941 and shortly after. This modest collection contains one of the earliest reviews of Michi Weglyn's *Years of Infamy* as a tribute to this aspect of post-Pearl Harbor consequences, a book still leader in its class as a study of the camp experience. But Mrs. Weglyn has called attention in her continuing researches to a remarkable memorandum to President Roosevelt from his Secretary of the Navy, Frank Knox, dated October 9, *1940* (to be found in PSF Box 5, Navy, in the Franklin Delano Roosevelt Library at Hyde Park, N.Y.) in which the Secretary listed fifteen "steps in preparation for war" which he recommended "be taken to impress the Japanese with the seriousness of our preparations." The 12th recommended "step" was: "Prepare plans for concentration camps." (Some friend of history in the past had attempted to blot out this recommendation from the memorandum, from the copy supplied this writer.) (Mrs. Weglyn has brought up another absorbing matter as worthy of further research: what was the origin of the product we call "Agent Orange," long since known for its employment as a defoliant in the Vietnam war of recent deplorable memory? Was it initially intended for utilization against Japan, much earlier, in an invasion which never took place? Anyone with even cursory acquaintance with American military and diplomatic papers recognizes after awhile that the U.S. code name in many of these documents for Japan is "Orange.")

If the general run of fighting men were not influenced by abstractions derived from listening to Foreign Policy Association radio talks, but were largely preoccupied by strategies of survival intermixed with their aims for revenge, what can we say of policy fabricated in and emanating from the highest levels? Probably the shortest definition of "statesmanship" was elucidated by the famed Johns Hopkins University geographer, Isaiah Bowman, "looking ahead." One must say that not much, if any, of this took place within the Roosevelt camp or that of his successor, Harry S. Truman. Most of the developments in the closing months of the war, and immediately after, struck with the characteristic catastrophe of the atom bomb, unprepared for and responded to with the usual confusion of makeshift temporizing and make-do which generally found the people in the highest places with the lowest jaws dropped in amazement at what happened, especially in the decade 1944-54. It was a time when shambles replaced even the primitive notions masquerading as 'policy' which had occasionally grazed the consciousness of the "statesmen." This slim compendium contains no paper on this affair, even though it is mentioned in various contexts along the way. (This writer attempted a rumination on the subject in an extended review of the book by the Oxford historian Christopher Thorne, *Allies of a Kind: The United States, Britain, and the War Against Japan, 1941-1945* [1978] in *Libertarian Review* for October, 1978, pp. 47-50). But this subject and that of the atomic bombing decision lie still deeply encumbered in contemporary politics, and a large part of such studies must be mainly speculative. (Did Mr. Truman *really* direct Mr. Stimson originally not to drop the atomic bombs on cities?)

For that matter, there is much of the Pacific War and its related Asian mainland campaigns still little told and in some instances untold, or just told. A case in point is the participation of American Japanese in the U.S. armed forces, a small part of which has long been exploited in the instance of those who took part in the European campaigns. But only in the last two years have we been able to learn that thousands upon thousands of Japanese-Americans took part in the war campaigns in the *Pacific,* on occasion even in combat against members of their families fighting in behalf of Imperial Japan. Only the book *Yankee Samurai* by the late Joseph D. Harrington (Detroit: Pettigrew, 1979) tells us about this. (Japanese-Americans were in the U.S. Pacific forces *before* Pearl Harbor; see the letter to the *Los Angeles Times* of November 23, 1981 by Yoshikazu Yamada, on his tour of duty as a draftee in service in the Philippines between November, 1941 and April, 1942 when he was airlifted to Australia on a stretcher after sustaining wounds in the fighting prior to the Corregidor surrender.)

It is obvious from what happened between 1945 and 1950 that the Roosevelt-Truman regime had no clear idea of what they wanted to prevail in China, after the massive campaign of talk and literature they had launched on the world prior to and during the war explaining how deeply involved Chinese affairs lay in American decisions in East Asia. Since the foundering of discussions over China policy was portrayed as the reason why a position was taken which precipitated the Japanese decision to go to war, the flabby performance after 'victory' was just another instance reinforcing the suspicion that there never was a serious policy for a postwar mainland East Asia, especially after it became obvious that the decayed and degenerate Euro-American colonial system opposed by the Japanese was going to self-destruct anyway.

But what was to be the 'new order' in Japan was certainly no clearer, and no improvement. John Hohenberg in a rather limp way in his book *New Era in the Pacific* (New York: Simon & Schuster, 1972), reminds us once more of "insurrections" in Far East American troop centers even *before* Japanese surrender on September 2, 1945, while stressing how anxious Americans were to return home rather than deal with the consequences and responsibilities stemming from their victory. Political leaders were only too happy to accommodate the armed forces.

What did the 'victors' want for Japan? Surely they did not expect the country to follow the Red course which seemed likely to swamp all of East Asia. They hardly could have listened to the likes of Guenther Stein tell them of the possibility of a Red Japan as a consequence of the efforts of the tiny Japanese Stalinist-Maoist cadre headed by Sanzo Nozaka, which had spent the war in Yenan, Despite the convoy of Maoist and Stalinist sympathizers resident in various American departments of government, nothing to advance this goal took place. Though defeated, it is important to note that the settlement of the Pacific War between Japan and the U.S.A. was a *negotiated* one, which could have been arrived at five or six months before the atom bombings, and the disintegration of Japanese society was not an objective under these stipulations. To be sure, various programs were later introduced, including the beheading of the Japanese wartime leader class via 'war crimes' trials, and the imposition of a strange 'constitution' to which the Japanese still adhere stubbornly, despite frequent efforts made to dissuade them into more 'realistic' courses since. (How strange it was that Stimson could have become so hotly indignant over regimes founded by force in 1931-32, and devised his famous "Doctrine" for non-recognition of same, and then becoming mute when such regimes proliferated in the same area in 1945 and after, under different auspices.)

Furthermore, the disastrous politics following the end of hostilities in the Pacific War in August, 1945, especially over the unresolved real estate issues of Korea and the old French Indo-China colonial preserve, already dissolved alarmingly in 1941, had consequences even more shocking and alarming to those who thought that after Pearl Harbor it was simply a matter of devastating Japan and retiring home to eternal peace and quiet. The return to influence of 'difficult' people such as the Japanese and the Thais in the subsequent decades might have been predicted.*

A major American building materials producer ran a most interesting full page advertisement in the October 8, 1980 issue of *Forbes Magazine,* titled "How America Became a Colony Again." Its obvious but unstated objective was the hope of overturning contemporary Japanese commercial and industrial success in the U.S.A., while expanding their purchases of American food and raw materials, the classic imperialist relationship. That Japan has essentially traded political independence for this economic advantage is rarely alluded to, and the 'one-world' conceptualists prefer to keep attention away from this situation. It is likely to remain a reality regardless of the distress it causes in America, until there is a major reversal in world affairs and Japan once more becomes an independent world power center. (Something of this sort also obtains in American-German relations, which many Germans would undoubtedly enjoy seeing coming to an end in the form of a united German power center again, but both the NATO and Warsaw Pacts, and the Helsinki agreements, exist to prevent that from happening. (And there *still* is no general peace treaty ending World War Two in Europe.)

The coming of the fortieth anniversary of the Japanese attack on Pearl Harbor, a brilliant tactical success for them in that it prevented the American Pacific Fleet from engaging in offensive action in behalf of the British and Dutch colonial powers in South East Asia already under a state of siege, which aid had already been pledged, and asked for, has been the occasion for the usual barrage of mindless journalistic flummery, totally lacking in political content and oozing with bravado and after-the-fact invented 'reasons' for it happening. To this day the majority of Americans have never been taught to relate the event to world politics and the consequence of the foreign policy of their revered President Roosevelt, whose 'day-of-infamy' diversionary oratory has usually been satisfactory over the years as an explanation of how it all came about. It has been his successors who have had to cope with the consequences of the war which ensued, and the progressively unsatisfactory resulting circumstances may account in part for the increasing vociferousness of the defense of Roosevelt and his Japanophobic regime by partisans who profess to this day to be so offended and appalled at the spread of revisionism in assaying this affair. In that sense we have gone 'beyond Pearl Harbor' to such a degree, and plunged into matters which seem to be so much more serious, if not dangerous, that it is understandable that so many contemporary Americans have responded to polls about the significance of Pearl Harbor to the effect that they are unaware why it should be remembered as of particular importance to United States history. If Asians ever return to a control over their affairs and their neighborhood as the Soviet Union is in theirs and the U.S.A. is in theirs, Pearl Harbor in future books may be stored away in an obscure footnote.

James J. Martin
Colorado Springs, Colorado
December, 1981.

---

*
Western histories seem compelled to treat Japan in the Second World War as utterly isolated, without allies, taking on the whole world. In its relations with Thailand, if mentioned at all, the impression is given that Thailand was an unwilling conquest, 'occupied' against its will, thus filling out the picture of an Asia totally committed against the Japanese. Ignored is the fact of permitted transit of Japanese troops across Thailand, thus outflanking the British in both their Burmese and Malay colonies. The British historian, Capt. B. H. Liddell Hart, in his massive *History of the Second World War* (1970) points out that there were only about 35,000 Japanese troops in Thailand when this occurred (hardly the forces needed to keep tranquil a land larger than Colorado and Wyoming combined, with a population in excess of thirty million.)

x

Ignored is that Thailand under its chief of state, Phibun Song-khram, not only authorized Japanese army passage across Thailand *the day after the Pearl Harbor attack,* but on January 25, 1942 declared war on both the United States and Great Britain and presumably acted as a full ally of Japan (Thailand and Japan were the only two clearly non-colonial lands in all of Asia in 1941). Contemporary materials in East Asia also tell their readers that even after defeat in 1945, Phibun returned to the premiership of Thailand on Nov. 8, 1947, and though temporarily ousted by wartime 'resistance' elements supportive of the Western colonial powers, took power again April 6, 1948, was recognized by the Truman regime in May, started joint operations with the American CIA in February 1949 and received back in October of that year the Thai gold valued at $44,000,000 which had been impounded by the USA while Thailand was an armed enemy, 1942-45. These and many other interesting facts are related in *Far Eastern Economic Review, Asia 1977 Yearbook* (Hong Kong, 1977), pp. 322-324.

James J. Martin

PEARL HARBOR:
Antecedents, Background and Consequences

PEARL HARBOR: Antecedents, Background and Consequences

> Wars are struggles between social organisms—called nations—for survival, struggles for the possession and use of the resources of the earth, for fertile fields, coal, oil, and iron deposits; for uranium mines, for seaports and waterways; for markets and trade routes; for military bases. No amount of understanding will alter or remove the *basis* of this struggle, any more than an understanding of the ocean's tides will diminish or terminate their flow.—Leslie A. White, *The Science of Culture* (New York: Farrar, Straus, 1949), p. 343.

There are *never* enough data to enable one to *prove* an unpopular historical thesis. An establishment, having anchored its line, predictably vilifies a rival and subjects those involved to ridicule and ultimately to personal detraction and traducement which goes far beyond that. This *ad hominem* denigration is expected to transfer to their intellectual product. And no matter what the latter put on the record, the former insist that it is not enough 'proof,' regardless of how flimsy or unconvincing was the'proof' used to create the establishment position.[2] Those seeking to revise this have to be made of stern stuff and willing to run the risk of a lifetime career of malicious disparagement. "Writing history is a dangerous trade," the redoubtable Charles A. Beard observed 40 years ago.

In the first few years after the end of World War Two, the supporters of the Roosevelt official camp scoffed at revisionism on the origins of American involvement in the war in 1941 as 'Chicago *Tribune* history,' (theirs might just as well have been called 'New York *Times* history'), mainly because of a continuing high degree of resentment toward Col. Robert R. McCormick, the publisher of the *Tribune,* who had resolutely opposed the Administration's war-drift, and given publicity to all challenges of the official apologia. These included two pioneer essays by John T. Flynn, "The Truth About Pearl Harbor" (October 22, 1944) and "The Final Secret of Pearl Harbor" (September 2, 1945). The other main reason for the name-calling was the publication in 1947 of the best book in the revisionist camp, *Pearl Harbor: The Story of the Secret War,*[3] by George Morgenstern, who was later to become the editor of the *Tribune*'s editorial page.

The chorus of derogation became even louder the following year, however, upon the publication of *President Roosevelt and the Coming of the War 1941* (New Haven: Yale University Press) by Beard, which confirmed the Morgenstern thesis and elaborated upon it in places. Though Beard was one of the most eminent American historians of this century, and was a former president of the most deeply rooted organization of the establishment historians, the American Historical Association, the incensed defenders of the Roosevelt innocence myth demonstrated that the credentials of no one were sufficiently prestigious to protect one from their character assassination. One could understand the patrician derision of and rudeness toward Beard by such as Professor Samuel Eliot Morison; after all, he had been given the rank of admiral and commissioned to write the official history of U.S. naval operations during the Second World War, and was therefore only showing his loyalty by defending his patron. But the ugly excesses of many others were utterly uncalled for, and represented gratuitous and contemptible scurrility toward an eminent scholar whom many of these same abusive people had not long before extolled and elevated to high honor within their own ranks.

It took awhile before the generalized snarling toward revisionism evolved into expectable criticism. Though Dr. Louis Morton, Chief of the Pacific Section of the U.S. Army Office of Military History, writing in the April, 1955 issue of the U.S. Naval Institute *Proceedings,* observed without evasive qualifications that revisionist writing on Pearl Harbor had achieved "the status of a mature historical interpretation" as early as 1948, it certainly was not respected as such in the latter year. The ferocity of the attack on revisionism and revisionists between 1945 and 1955 is in a class by itself in the history of history in recent times; in the following ten years it subsided slowly.

The likelihood of a showdown war in the Far East between Japan and the Caucasian colonial powers sometime in the first half of the 20th century had been the subject of a vast literary enterprise long before the war of 1939 broke out. It had been common speculation after the 1905 humiliation of Imperial Russia by Japan, the first modern defeat of a European power by an Asiatic one. As early as 1909 Old Asia Hands such as Homer Lea were predicting a collision between the U.S. and Japan, and the tension grew far heavier after 1918, when Japan emerged as a major factor in Far East affairs.

The first World War and the revolution in global power it inaugurated, accentuating the importance of the USA everywhere, and diminishing that of Great Britain, and especially Russia, in the Far East, brought about secondary revolutions. One of these, growing out of the new closeness between Britain and the USA, seen in many different developments, even in the re-writing of American histories in the 1920s with a far more mellow appreciation of England (which Charles Grant Miller so bitterly attacked in his *The Poisoned Loving-Cup: United States Histories Falsified Through Pro-British Propaganda In the Sweet Name of Amity* [1928]), involved a profound turnaround in East Asia. American imperial interests had long sought to wreck the Anglo-Japanese Alliance of January 30, 1902. The intimate political involvement of the Anglo-American war regimes in 1917-1918 provided the major change in climate for the initiation of the assault on it. During the Washington Naval Conference of 1921-1922 the dismantling of this Anglo-Japanese alliance was achieved, and from then on Britain was gradually steered into the train of American confrontation of Japan, though England's policy makers continued to show some reluctance in changing to a program which aimed at ultimately destroying Japan, for decades viewed as a counter-weight to Russia in the Far East. Worse still, after razing the old position toward Japan, the USA officially backed off for a time from supporting the new.

At a time when the disarmament ploys of the newly-created League of Nations late in 1920 consisted of pressure on Japan to reduce their naval strength while Great Britain and the U.S. were bent on increasing theirs, the Japanese home front opinion was incensed enough. But particularly infuriating was the almost simultaneous passage by the California State Legislature, by a 3-1 margin, of an "Anti-Alien Land Law," excluding Japanese from the right to own land in the state, a move which other states started to copy. Many Japanese regarded this as a stinging racial insult and were not long in letting everyone know. An Associated Press report from Tokyo on November 16, 1920 informed Americans that "The students' societies of three of Tokyo's private universities have organized a meeting to be held tonight to discuss the question, 'Shall Japan Fight America?' "[4]

Following the takeover in Korea and the establishment of a corner in North China, the Japanese expansion into Manchuria in 1931 signalled several things. This represented a major challenge to the status quo in Asia which grew out of the World War I settlements, as well as an indication that sooner or later an Asia-for-the-Asiatics movement was bound to explode into a martial cataclysm. That not only happened: its late stages are taking place right now.

British efforts to erect a road block to Japan in the League of Nations were not successful, and they failed to get support from the U.S., not a member, even though Pres. Herbert Hoover had in Henry L. Stimson[5] as Secretary of State a sophisticated and aristocratic Japanophobe. Hoover's successor in the White House, Franklin D. Roosevelt, in March, 1933, brought no change in this hands-off policy. As if to emphasize this, in a nationwide radio address on Dec. 28 of that same year, front-paged across the land, Roosevelt announced that not only did the U.S. not intend to join the League but that it was committed to "a definite policy" of opposition "to intervention in the affairs of other nations."[6] The subsequent passage by Congress of the Neutrality Acts of 1935 and 1937 seemed to be evidence of the hardest kind that this policy was real, not superficial talk.

But at the moment U.S. policy seemed incapable of being altered in the direction of new involvement in international wars, a subtle shift was underway in that direction. Critics such as Beard pointed this out even as it was starting to take place. He and others emphasized that the failure of the domestic program of FDR, especially the collapse of the effort to cure the chronic unemployment of the 1930s (Gottfried Haberler, Professor of Economics at Harvard and a President of the American Economic Association, called the failure of the New Deal a policy disaster "unparalleled in other countries"), was responsible for the Administration diverting attention from this by increased concentration on foreign affairs (it was Shakespeare who had Henry IV advise his son to "busy giddy minds with foreign quarrels.")

Roosevelt tested public reaction to a change from neutrality to 'collective security' in his famous Chicago speech of Oct. 5, 1937 but was repelled by the public coolness to his suggested involvement in the growing world tensions, and abandoned this idea. And when war broke out in September, 1939 the national policy was still neutrality. But under this official curtain there now took place a long string of moves which amounted to *de facto* participation in the war on the side of Britain. As *The Economist* of London summarized it a few years ago (reprinted in the New York *Times* for July 2, 1971), "When President Roosevelt told the Americans in the 1940 election that 'I shall say it again and again and again: your boys are not going to be sent into any foreign wars,' he had already committed the United States to a huge program of military aid to Britain, and he had drawn up the 'Rainbow' contingency plans for a simultaneous war with Germany and Japan, and was soon to slap on Japan the embargoes which some people still believe pushed the Japanese into their attack on Pearl Harbor." (More will be said about 'Rainbow' later.) A little over 13 months after Roosevelt's memorable Navy Day 'again, and again and again' speech,[7] at the Boston Navy Yard on October 30, 1940 the USA was at war with Japan.

The road to Pearl Harbor was entered upon resolutely in 1941. For 25 years after the war a numerous and powerful group of pro-Roosevelt spokesmen vigorously denied that he had ever made any moves in the direction of war, and sought peace exclusively in the period between September, 1938 and Dec. 7, 1941. However, a new generation of Roosevelt defenders is far more frank in admitting that in the year before actual American involvement FDR strove mightily and assiduously to become embroiled in World War II, which is unequivocally supported by British government documents and papers not made public until Jan. 1, 1972 (see New York *Times*, Jan 2. 1972).

After failing to lure the Germans into an act which would justify entry,[8] or to execute the proper maneuvers to take advantage of an act that did,[9] the efforts finally paid off in the Pacific. A *Fortune* magazine poll published in January, 1946, a few months after the end of hostilities, asked the question, "Do you think the USA did or did not deliberately provoke Japan into making war against us?" Nearly 30% of the respondents either agreed the attack on Hawaii was provoked, or were sufficiently dubious about it to the point of refusing to accept the Administration's pose of innocence. It is revealing that this question was not asked again; in view of the revisionist publications of 1947 and after, the total would surely have been greater.

There are two classes of facts relative to the Pearl Harbor story: a) those on the public record in the period before the attack and b) those revealed by one or another of the nine Pearl Harbor investigations. There is a masterly chapter on this latter subject by Percy L. Greaves, Jr. in the symposium edited by Harry Elmer Barnes, *Perpetual War for Perpetual Peace* (1953).[10] It is difficult to discuss the former without bringing in the latter as one goes along.

The worsening of U.S. relations with Japan in the last six months of 1941 presaged serious trouble. The abrogation of the 1911 trade treaty with the Japanese was followed by what has sometimes been called the "Japanese Pearl Harbor," the freezing of all Japanese assets in the U.S. by presidential order on July 26, and the embargoing of materials crucial to Japanese survival. Japan, at that time a nation of some seventy million people crammed into an area the size of California but of which only one-seventh was arable and possessing the natural resources of the state of Mississippi, had long before become dependent on imports of raw materials and vast international trade.

Japanese trade with the U.S. exceeded that of mainland Asia combined, but tariff walls had been steadily constricting it. Now there was this abrupt halt, an act of economic warfare of the most obvious sort. It hurt the anti-war, peace and negotiation moderates in Japan, and led to the success of the war party and the decision to move sharply upon the French, British and Dutch Asian colonies to the south of Japan to get by war what was denied to them in peace.

Hawaii was on the flank of this movement, and the U.S. Pacific Fleet, having been recently based there, comprised the only threat to Japanese success in enveloping all the European colonies with their rich troves of oil, rubber and scores of other desperately needed products. A move by the U.S. Navy in support of the colonial powers would have made the Japanese invasion a precarious undertaking.

There is no doubt about the genuineness of Japanese efforts to seek a peaceful understanding with the U.S. right down to Pearl Harbor week. Top Administration figures were able to read the most secret Japanese messages starting in August, 1940 when an Army cryptanalytic team, utilizing the ideas of Harry L. Clark, broke the top Japanese diplomatic code, known among Americans as "Purple." A machine was constructed to decode "Purple," and the decoded traffic was designated "Magic." The subsequent location of "Purple" machines is fundamental to an understanding of the reason for the general ignorance of the state of U.S.-Japanese relations in the closing weeks of 1941: there was never a "Purple" machine sent to any branch of counter-intelligence at the Pearl Harbor base, nor was anyone there given access to the decoded "Magic" traffic. (One should consult on the above matters Ladislas Farago's *The Broken Seal*,[11] essentially another Administration apologia but which makes numerous admissions of revisionist positions.)

Of course the general public in the U.S. had not the faintest idea anything of this sort had taken place until after the war, although this code-breaking nearly became a factor in the 1944 election.[12] In the meantime, backing a hard line of pressure by the policy makers under FDR, the latter simultaneously demanded of Japan a number of concessions regarding its conduct in China. Since mid-1937 Japan had been waging a full-scale war there against the regime headed by Chiang Kai-shek and also against a large Communist enclave directed by Mao Tse-tung. The latter had been under formation since the 1920s and already occupied a portion of northwest China as large as France, and with a population of 75 millions. But few Americans were aware of it even at this late date (1941), and the Administration paid no formal attention to Maoist communism in China. It sought only to get the Japanese to terminate their war against Chiang, but on terms so humiliating that it was once suggested that if they had been presented to

Andorra or San Marino, even these tiny lands would have declared war on the U.S., let alone when advanced on a take-it-or-else basis to a tough and successful opponent such as Japan.

The amazing thing is that the Japanese were willing to accede to so many of the American demands concerning China and persisted in trying to negotiate their rival clashes of interest so long. In retrospect, the exaggerated concern for the integrity of China on the part of the Roosevelt regime insofar as it involved Japanese incursions sounded hollow when it was observed that several European countries, and also the U.S., enjoyed special geographical spheres of influence in China themselves.

[It is far from clear or agreed upon what Roosevelt and Hull, and to a lesser degree Churchill, expected to emerge in the Far East upon the reduction of Japan. Neither the colonial *status quo ante* nor the mainly theoretical international liberal capitalist dream of the era before 1914 were likely to prevail or materialize. Though the USA starting in May 1941 and the British in July of that same year plainly intended to renounce the extraterritorial rights they enjoyed in China (realized by their joint re-negotiation of the new 'equal' treaties with Chiang on January 11, 1943), there was no evidence that they would enjoy any previous economic advantages, even though it appeared Britain would cling to Hong Kong.

If there was any of the mirage of the Open Door still drifting across Sec. Hull's consciousness, it should have been dissipated by the publication in China on March 10, 1943 of Chiang's book *China's Destiny,* which went into more than 200 printings in just that year alone, followed shortly thereafter by Chiang's *Chinese Economic Theory;* these were read by nearly every literate Chinese. Though not generally available in English translations until 1947, they both drew much outside attention anyway, most of the comment in the USA being very critical. The general hostility in these books toward Western ways and concepts, including most of their economic traditions, made it evident that Western influences in the Far East could be expected to decline even more rapidly after the war than they had been doing before.

And the promise of expanded civil war against Mao Tse-tung in these volumes infuriated the various enthusiasts for Stalin and Mao in the West even more than those hoping for a restoration of the 19th century in Asia. The Reds and their many fellow travelers knew their priorities; the success of Mao was totally dependent upon the expulsion of Japan from mainland Asia. Once this was achieved, they were at liberty to abandon their wartime "spirit of Tehran" and concentrate their full venom on Chiang. Causing a diversion by feigning horror about Chiang's 'anti-Western' views for the future was part of their successful strategy. (Taiwan under Chiang after 1949 developed in a way far from the recipes he laid out for China's future in 1943.)

In this light, it does not appear that the Anglo-American defenders of the past in the Far East had any real choice; Japan and Chiang were both smashed, only to see a triumphant Maoist Communism create a mainland China which in retrospect made either of the wrecked orders appear to be a genial milieu of mutual cooperation and prosperity.]

In the meantime the Japanese sweep southward to envelop the European colonies was taking firmer shape, in the early fall of 1941. At this point it is pertinent to put on the record one of the basic differences of the establishment and the revisionists concerning the Pearl Harbor attack. The former stress unduly the neglect of the commanders of the armed forces in Hawaii of a succession of local 'warnings' of the coming attack in the hour or two before the Japanese planes appeared over the Honolulu base.[13] The revisionists maintain that this is a diversion to blur out the realities of the total situation, and want to know why no solid, clearly-stated and unevasive warning of looming Japanese assault was not made as early as Oct. 9, 1941, and frequently thereafter, let alone the peculiar and persistent neglect to supply the Hawaii commanders with a "Purple" machine, of which there were several. Possession of the latter would have made it possible to read the Japanese diplomatic traffic themselves and thus be aware of the dramatic disintegration of Japanese-American relations.

As to the above date: beginning Sept. 24, 1941 the Japanese consul general in Hawaii began, on request, to send back to Japan detailed maps of the disposition of the American ships in Pearl Harbor, sometimes twice a week. The first was intercepted and decoded, and distributed Oct. 9. These became known as the "Kita," or "Bomb Plot" messages, and they increasingly and obviously pinpointed Pearl as the attack site in case diplomatic negotiations broke down. The commanders in Hawaii were never informed of these, right down to the day before the attack, when one of them was noted to include information that the details of ship disposition should also be flashed to Japanese vessels or submarines offshore. Key personnel in Washington examined this at 2:30 p.m. on Dec. 6; Hawaii was not notified.

Meanwhile the evidence that the diplomatic negotiations with the U.S. might founder led the Japanese to warn their diplomatic corps around the world that a deadline of Nov. 29 would prevail, and that if no agreement had been reached by then, things would start to happen. There were no signs of compromise in the pronouncements of Sec. of State Cordell Hull; they actually got more abusive rather than conciliatory. And by now the Roosevelt cabinet included the anti-Japan hardliner Stimson as Secretary of War, whose diary later revealed his hope for a Japanese first-strike to provide an excuse for full scale participation in the war. Such vaguely-written messages to the Hawaiian commanders as were sent late in November suggested possible Japanese attacks in the Philippines, or warned them to take precautions against local sabotage, but never mentioned the possibility of a move to destroy the Honolulu-based Pacific Fleet.

The rejection by the Japanese of Hull's 'ultimatum' of Nov. 26[14] led to a sharp increase of traffic in the "Purple" code, including notification to worldwide Japanese diplomatic stations to destroy their codebooks and code machines on Dec. 1 and 2. One of the many amazing reactions in Washington to the most obvious Japanese preparations for war some days before December 7 was the casual and unconcerned response to this particular action. Admiral Royal E. Ingersoll, assistant chief of naval operations in the Navy Department, was to declare before the Joint Congressional Committee on the Investigation of the Pearl Harbor Attack on

February 11, 1946, "When you tell diplomats to burn codes, that means war." This is not always the case, but in the context of everything else happening in early December, 1941 it surely was so. Washington authorities later in the cover-up tried to exculpate themselves by asserting that the commanders in Hawaii had been told of the code-burning order, but these same authorities did not consider it an irretrievable step toward war at the time, nor did they give any indications of feeling that way to Hawaii. The message the Hawaii commanders did *not* get, however, was the crucially critical "East Wind, Rain" message of the 4th, definitely indicating war with the U.S.A. This final war decision by the Japanese government was disguised as a false weather report, sent out by Japanese Morse Code, and not on the radio channels, and was picked up by Navy intelligence in Cheltenham, Maryland.

The story of the suppression of this message and the effort to maintain that it was never intercepted, on the part of the FDR regime's spokesmen, during the subsequent investigations, has produced an almost booklength narrative itself. Had the official coverup contingent been able to crack Captain Laurence F. Safford, chief of Navy communications intelligence, on this matter, they might have made great headway in setting the scene for the innocence myth, but that they were never able to do. Captain Safford maintained stubbornly over a substantial period of time and after repeated interrogation that such a dispatch had been intercepted, decoded, and widely distributed. That all copies vanished is not to be wondered at; it was the fate of other documents bearing substantial consequence to the situation in Washington.

By now the Japanese aircraft carrier task force with its complement of bombers was on its way from Japan, calculated to arrive 200 miles from Hawaii, from which point the surprise assault would begin, on the 7th. Going on simultaneously was the massive naval operations to the south along the coast of Asia, destined to result in swift occupation of what are now known as Thailand, Vietnam and Indonesia. Operations near this latter land, known then as the Dutch East Indies, triggered another and probably more significant series of events, which in most ways makes the Pearl Harbor attack a supporting incidental, since the former involved the U.S. in the Pacific War *four days before* the Hawaii bombing.

Between January and March, 1941 joint staff conferences between the U.S. and the British took place in Washington. These were extended the following month to include the Dutch, in meetings held in Singapore. Out of all this came the ABCD agreement, committing the conferees to a mutual agreement to fight the Japanese in Asia if their forces crossed a geographic line of 100° East and 10° North, which approximated the northerly extremity of the DEI. Though the agreement was only verbal, the British and Dutch took it as an irreversible commitment, while US armed forces drew up a general contingency war plan in harmony with it, which became known as WPL 46. The entire agreement was known as "Rainbow 5," and the part involving the Dutch was known as "Rainbow A-2."

Around 5 p.m. on Thursday, Dec. 4, Australian time (Dec. 3,

Washington time), the U.S. military attache in Melbourne, Australia, Col. Van S. Merle-Smith, and his aide, Lt. Robert H. O'Dell, were invited to a conference at which were present the head of the Australian air force and the Dutch liaison officer to Australia from Batavia (now Djakarta). Col. Merle-Smith was informed that the chief of the Dutch Navy in Asia had notified them that the Japanese had crossed the magic line (see above) and that the Dutch had put into operation the ABCD and Rainbow-5 (A-2) plans, and were expecting help from the U.S. Navy in repelling this Japanese action. So—the USA was involved in the Pacific phase of World War II whether they approved of this or not. That the general public knew nothing of this or that the FDR regime did not actually sign any documents involving the USA in this arrangement are irrelevant; the other signatories to the agreement took it very seriously, and expected the USA to honor the commitment.

There is a lengthy story involving the efforts to keep this news from the high dignitaries in Washington. Ultimately it made its way there via Hawaii in encoded form, which should have reached Washington in the early evening of Dec. 4, Washington time. The decoded message never came back to Hawaii, and a copy did not surface in Washington until seven hours after the bombing of Pearl on the 7th. Its suppression for two and possibly three days is one of the unexplained mysteries concerning the whole matter of Pearl Harbor warnings. As Commander Hiles, the closest student of the Merle-Smith episode, puts it, "Encoded messages from military attaches in time of crisis such as this one do not lie around neglected unless for ulterior purposes of no honest portent or through gross negligence." The facts surrounding this electrifying incident went on record in an investigation in 1944 but nothing was ever done to bring about any further knowledge about it. Hiles's summary of this matter in the Chicago *Tribune* for Dec. 7, 1966 deserves study.[15]

The 18 hours preceding the actual bombing of Pearl Harbor have been the subject of many hundreds of pages in more than a score of books. The main act of the drama involves the famous 14-part diplomatic message from Tokyo to its ambassador in Washington, in essence a notice of formal breaking of diplomatic relations. The first 13 parts were intercepted and decoded by the early hours of the evening of the 6th, copies of which were sent to the President and to the military and naval chiefs, Gen. George Marshall and Adm. Harold Stark. Commander L. R. Schultz, who delivered the copy to FDR around 9:30 p.m., reported later that the President read part of it in his presence and exclaimed, "This means war!" Gen. Marshall could not be found (a fantastic story in itself), and Adm. Stark was finally located attending a theater performance. But nothing was done all that night to alert the forces in Hawaii.

The timing of the delivery of the 14th part, which the recipients of the first 13 were told would be around 1 p.m., Washington time, the next day (Dec. 7), made it evident that this would contain the actual notice that relations were formally ruptured, even though this could easily be divined from the context of the previous parts. Time of delivery in Washington would thus be around 7 a.m. Honolulu time. Though the 14th part was received and decoded by 10 a.m. in Washington, still nothing was done to warn the Hawaii commanders all the morning of the 7th until nearly noon. Ignoring the separate FBI and Navy radio senders and a scrambler telephone, Gen. Marshall had a message to Adm. Kimmel and Gen. Short sent by commercial Western Union cable, which was not delivered to them until hours after the attack, ironically by a Japanese messenger.

Navy Secretary Knox, the commencement speaker at the accelerated Naval Academy's 1942 commencement twelve days after Pearl Harbor, asserted, "There is no question at all that half an hour's warning of the approach of the Japanese planes would have made all the difference in the world."[16] Harry Elmer Barnes in his *The Final Story of Pearl Harbor* (1968) quotes Commander Hiles' view that if a strong warning had been supplied to Adm. Kimmel even as late as 9:30 a.m. Washington time, this would have provided sufficient time to have the major ships sortie from the harbor, to put up the fighter planes on alert, and to have the anti-aircraft guns readied for defense of the base. And Gordon W. Prange has shown in his *Tora! Tora! Tora!*[17] that the Japanese commander of the carrier-based strike force had orders to call off the attack and return home if Pearl showed signs of readiness to repel the attack

At 7:55 a.m. on Sunday, December 7, 1941 the Japanese bombers struck the Pearl Harbor naval base and the Army and Navy airfields on Oahu. Eight battleships and several smaller craft were destroyed or put out of action for a long time (it was fortunate that the aircraft carriers and submarines were away on maneuvers), and most of the military aircraft were destroyed on the ground. Nearly three thousand American soldiers, sailors and marines were killed and many others wounded, and the total damage wrought by the attack was in the many millions of dollars.

For this price the Roosevelt Administration was able to enter World War II via the Pacific, and ultimately into the entire global conflagration, with nearly universal popular support. In the absence of a Japanese attack and in view of prior Dutch action in invoking Rainbow A-2, the Roosevelt regime would have been caught in the same flypaper which eventually entangled Lyndon Johnson and Vietnam. Having to explain to an increasingly sullen populace how we had become involved in an Asian war which a vast majority wanted no part of (as public opinion polls to the very day of the attack demonstrated), followed by a steady slipping and sliding into expanded hostilities, would have resulted in a major domestic political upheaval in due course.

As it was, Roosevelt and his bi-partisan war administration narrowly escaped a major scandal resulting from a comprehensive investigation, had it taken place right at the start. Talk of a Congressional investigation in the immediate aftermath of the attack undoubtedly galvanized Administration efforts to smother it. Roosevelt managed to get assurances from the chairmen of both the House and Senate Naval Affairs Committees, Carl Vinson (Dem.-Ky.) and David I. Walsh (Dem.-Mass.), that he would have their full cooperation and that they would launch no investigations. But there still was a threatened 'independent investigation' in Congress, largely urged by Senator Robert A. Taft (Rep.-Ohio). To head this off, Roosevelt on the evening of December 16, 1941 named a five-man board to conduct an investigation of the Pearl Harbor disaster, headed by Associate Justice of the Supreme Court Owen J. Roberts, assisted by two Navy and two Army officers. They met for the first time in War Sec. Stimson's office on the next day,[18] and it was formally constituted as the Roberts Commission by Executive Order the day after that.

It was not clearly understood what they were going to investigate, and it was generally not known until after the war that they had been given the authority to examine "only the circumstances of the attack and not what happened in Washington," as David Lawrence was to relate.[19] But the big job was to rush through an inquiry of some sort and have it completed before a rival and contradictory challenge might be forthcoming from the Congress.

The day after the creation of the Roberts Commission, Sen. Taft delivered an address before the Executive Club in Chicago, denouncing the notion that a Pearl Harbor investigation should be left entirely to the Executive Department, and again asking that a Congressional inquiry take place. Taft especially wanted to know if Sec. Hull had told Navy Sec. Knox the full contents of his 'ultimatum' to the Japanese of November 26, and "Did Sec. Knox communicate to Adm. Kimmel [in command at Pearl Harbor] that we had sent an ultimatum to Japan which in all probability they would not accept?"[20]

In retrospect, Sen. Taft's call for an investigation of Pearl Harbor independent of that which the Roosevelt Administration was hurriedly patching and stitching together was an act of high political courage. The major difficulty was the absence of a popular base from which he might have secured reassurance and support. Stunned by the Japanese attack and the belligerent roar of the Administration, and its overwhelming back-up by a pro-war communications media, there were few in a psychological position wherein they might have expressed reservations about what was happening. The immediate response was one of incoherent accommodation. The result was the absence of any kind of formal policy opposition, of which there was at least a vocal vestige in Great Britain.

The prompt demise of the most formidable anti-involvement organization, the America First Committee, was surely the crushing final blow to any hopes Taft might have had to securing a modicum of public support. What might have happened had the AFC remained as a sort of 'his majesty's loyal opposition,' so to speak, has been mulled over for decades by students of the time. Even at the moment, there were those who thought that ultimately such a force might have had a profound influence over the way the war was fought after the U.S.A. became a full belligerent, and that its settlement would have been immensely different from what transpired in 1945. As for the Pearl Harbor affair, a vigorous and growing America First Committee in the early year of the war might have been the concentration point leading to an investigation with results of considerable gravity to all involved. As Robert R. Young, the railroad magnate who was one of the founders of the AFC, put it in a letter to Barnes on June 2, 1953:[21]

I happened to be one of the three dissenting voices when the directors of the America First Committee voted to disband on the Wednesday after Pearl Harbor. I felt then and still feel that if the Committee could only have been kept going, some of these people who will become national heroes could have been made to pay for their sins by their liberty or even their lives. If the Republicans had not been equally corrupted they could have had the whole damned crowd in jail.

It soon became obvious that the Roberts Commission was uninterested in anything fundamental. Confining themselves almost entirely to the immediate circumstances attending the Japanese assault, the Commission produced in a matter of 20 days a 51-page report which tacked the blame for it all on the Army and Navy commanders in Hawaii, General Walter C. Short and Admiral Husband E. Kimmel, for having failed to take the necessary protective precautions. It was released the evening of January 24, 1942 and made public the following day. [22]

The Roberts Commission report was a temporary anaesthetic, providing a mild analgesic to the troubled public for awhile. The wider investigations of Pearl were to come later; in the meantime the Administration had a war to fight, and little was allowed to interfere with this. The almost total collapse of domestic opposition after the events of December 7, 1941 made this ever so much easier to conduct. The long global upheaval which followed resulted in planetary dislocations so profound that over thirty years after it ended formally, the unresolved consequences were still the major aspects of world politics.

Space prevents any substantial review of the consequences of the horrendous conflict in the Pacific after December 7, 1941. Ignoring for other considerations any discussion of the credibility gap involved in the official explanation of the circumstances which led up to Pearl, it is obvious that a vast amount of unsettled business remains on the scene even 34 years later. Though Roosevelt was able to "pull ashore the corpse of the British Empire," as the Baltimore *Sun's* inimitable Henry L. Mencken put it after the war, the nearly total dissolution of the colonial system was the first observable consequence of a war which was obviously expected to preserve and continue it. Though Japan's expansion was checked and reversed and the Japanese Empire destroyed, the principal result for Asia was the unleashing of Communism on a mighty scale, and it was Communism which was ultimately the primary winner.

The attempt by the USA at incredible expense during the last quarter of a century to restore a balance of power in the Far East has not been successful, and the future is clouded with the possibility of a number of other serious disturbances. If statesmanship can be defined as the ability to look ahead, it may be admitted without much danger of being controverted that there was not much of it involved in the conduct of American relations with the Far East in the decade which had as its culmination the December 7, 1941 disaster at Pearl Harbor and the ferocious four-year war that ensued. In one sense it is fortunate for Americans that only the fiascoes of Korea and Vietnam have followed. For things might have been much worse. [23]

The full impact of the saturation conquest in the Far East has yet to be felt by Americans, even though the swift overrunning of much of it by Communist regimes, and the collapse of the colonialism which largely was the reason the U.S.A. became embroiled in the war in the first place, have certainly indicated the likely direction things will take for a long time. The price paid by the U.S.A. for the continued control of Japan has been very high, but what has befallen the colonial powers of Britain, France and Holland after the 'triumph' of 1945 almost defies description. It was Dryden who wrote, "Ev'n victors are by victories undone."

NOTES

[1]This essay was prepared at the request of a features editor of the Colorado Springs *Sun* for publication on December 7, 1975, the 34th anniversary of the Pearl Harbor attack. It was written under severe word limitations, and although initially accepted, it was turned down by the editor in chief with the recommendation that it be compressed into about a third of the size tendered. Since it was felt that it was gravely condensed already, and likely to encourage a superficial approach to the problem if further reduced, the matter was allowed to lapse. Substituted for it was an I-was-there tidbit with the emphasis on human-interest, journalism's unerring recourse in a situation where a serious investigation into something might take place, as H. L. Mencken remarked in 1946 while surveying the reportage of World War Two. The assumptions, in reproducing vignettes from the memory of a sailor a few decks down on an exploding ship, or of a housewife viewing the carnage from afar from a rooftop, neither of whom may have the faintest inkling as to the history of 20th century Japanese-American relations, and even less of the political and diplomatic tensions between the two countries in the eight weeks before the bombing of December 7, 1941, were that the diversion of attention to emotional decorations will be more entertaining, and that one should not expect casual newspaper skimmers to devote an hour to a serious examination of the essentials of the event. The opportunity for rococo embellishments is another matter, and represents an ancient penchant of the race for imaginary enhancement of facts, something which Ulysses and his crew came to understand.

The version published in this symposium has been expanded beyond what was originally submitted for publication as mentioned above, mainly with minor illustrative material. Selected items of documentation, originally omitted, result in considerable enlargement.

[2]As Harry Elmer Barnes commented sardonically, the last-ditch defenders of the total innocence of Franklin D. Roosevelt and his major political, military and naval administrators virtually required of the revisionists that they come up with a letter of confession by FDR which contained not only an admission of having planned the Pearl Harbor attack but of having been in the lead Japanese plane that dropped the bombs.

As the most prolific writer on the subject from the point of view of the total situation involving the Establishment official apologists and the revisionists, one should consult at least the following of Barnes's writings covering the two decades after the end of World War II: *The Struggle Against the Historical Blackout* (9th ed., privately printed, 1951); *The Court Historians Versus Revisionism* (2nd rev. and enlarged ed., privately printed, 1952);"Revisionism and the Promotion of Peace," *Liberation* (Summer, 1958), pp. 4-16; "Revisionism Revisited," *Liberation* (Summer, 1959), pp. 22-27; *Blasting the Historical Blackout* (privately printed, 1963); *Revisionism and Brainwashing* (privately printed, 1963); "The Public Stake in Revisionism," *Rampart Journal* (Summer, 1967), pp. 19-41. Essential to an overview of the consequences of the two great wars of the twentieth century is the compendium compiled by Barnes, with the assistance of several other revisionists, titled *Select Bibliography of Revisionist Books Dealing with the Two World Wars and Their Aftermath* (2nd. rev. ed., privately printed, 1958, with mimeographed supplement, March, 1966).

[3]New York: Devin-Adair, 425 pp. In a private memorandum, Barnes wrote of this book as "the first full-sized contribution to the 'period of Enlightenment' " beginning on the subject of revelations on World War Two, which he thought would far exceed what had been made on World War One, in which he had taken a prominent part; "when the full truth about the responsibility for the Second World War is revealed, the story will make my *Genesis of the World War* seem like an evening lullaby for an Old Ladies' Home."

[4]On Viscount Ishii's resentful response to the League of Nations Disarmament Committee on its version of what the postwar naval world should look like, see New York *Times*, December 12, 1920, p. 1. On the report of the Tokyo 'debate topic' growing out of the California land law, see New York *Times*, November 17, 1920, p. 17; Colorado Springs *Gazette*, November 17, 1920, p. 1.

[5]Stimson was an American analogue of the "Old Inja Hands" popularly related to Clive, Raffles, Kipling, the Bengal Lancers, "Chinese" Gordon, Lord Kitchener, Winston Churchill and other romantic types identified with the high-water mark of British Asian and African colonial imperialism, and which are still sentimentalized in film and print. When Roosevelt turned away from anti-war 'isolationists' in his own party and selected aged Republicans eager for battle in Asia such as Stimson, whom he made Secretary of War, and Frank Knox, few if any called attention to Stimson's World War One combat experience as a field artillery officer, and his two-year stint as Governor General of the Philippines between 1927 and 1929 at the time General Douglas MacArthur was there in command of the U.S. Armed forces. It was turn-of-the-century colonial-style thinking among the highest level of Anglo-American top leadership in Asia which led directly to the string of disasters of the early months of the expansionist stage of the Pacific War; the Japanese were not "fuzzywuzzies," and they were not intimidated by a "whiff of the grape."

Knox, Secretary of the Navy, was no less enthusiastic for war than Stimson, though he entertained some inhibitions which the latter obviously did not share. In Knox's office one wall was nearly covered by a huge German swastika flag which had been taken from the German ship *Odenwald* when it was apprehended and taken into custody by the *U.S.S. Omaha* in the South Atlantic, in mid-November, 1941. The ship was running the British blockade, and the American interference created a very tense situation, there being no state of war between the U.S.A. and Germany. There was a serious problem for the American captain of the *Omaha* in engaging in a patently warlike act in behalf of the British. Eventually he rationalized the action by reporting that he had considered the *Odenwald* a "suspected slave trader." Samuel Eliot Morison related this story without even blushing or winking in the first volume of his *History of United States Naval Operations, The Battle of the Atlantic September 1939-May 1943*, p. 84. The presence of the German flag in Sec. Knox's office and where it came from was related in an Associated Press dispatch found in the Colorado Springs *Evening Telegraph*, November 26, 1941, p. 2.

[6]Ironically, Roosevelt's resolute 'isolationist' speech was delivered on the 75th anniversary of the birth of Woodrow Wilson, patron of internationalism, father of the League of Nations, and in whose cabinet Roosevelt had been assistant secretary of the Navy. Among the things Roosevelt declared were no longer unilateral United States obligations was "the maintenance of constitutional government in other nations," while he credited Wilson with another policy innovation, at least in theory, which he was giving renewed support, the promise that the U.S. would "never again seek one additional foot of territory by conquest." See story and full text of this speech in New York *Times*, December 29, 1933, pp. 1, 3; it was front-paged under a dramatic headline in the Colorado Springs *Gazette* for December 29, 1933.

[7]The pertinent part of the President's speech ran as follows:

> And while I am talking to you mothers and fathers, I give you one more assurance. I have said this before, and I shall say it again and again and again. Your boys are not going to be sent into any foreign wars. They are going into training to form a force so strong that, by its very existence, it will keep the threat of war away from our shores. The purpose of our own defense is defense.

It might be argued that the key word in this was "sent." There was nothing said about those who might *volunteer* to enter the combat war zones. Scores of U.S. pilots fought in the Royal Air Force over England and Europe in the 10 months before formal U.S. belligerence, and are credited with shooting down 73 German planes in that period. There was a similar contingent in the Royal Canadian Air Force, and over ten thousand volunteers from the U.S. in the Canadian army during that time. A detachment of American Marines arrived in Northern Ireland to train in June, 1941, and were established at a base built by American civilian workers out of American materials. On these and related matters of some interest see David Lampe, "Over-Paid, Over-Sexed, Over-Here," in the *Sunday Times Magazine* of London for December 4, 1966.

[8]An interesting sidelight to the attempt to provoke Japanese hostility in the Pacific is the book by Admiral (ret.) Kemp Tolley, *The Cruise of the Lanikai: Incitement to War* (Annapolis, Md.: Naval Institute Press, 1973). On December 5, 1941 this little sailing ship was hastily commissioned in the U.S. Navy at Manila and then-Lieut. Tolley was placed in command, with instructions to put to sea as a part of a "defensive information patrol" in the face of the

Japanese navy cruising down the Philippine coast on its way to southeast Asian points. Tolley first wrote of this strange expedition in the U.S. Naval Institute *Proceedings* in the issues for September, 1962 and October, 1963. He noted that he had a radio that did not work, and even had he observed anything of importance he could not have relayed the news to anyone in any case. It was his eventual conviction that his real mission was to bring about its attack by the Japanese, thus providing an excuse for the Administration to enter World War II by way of the Pacific "back door." The lengthy article in the Chicago *Tribune* for December 7, 1967 titled "U.S. Entered World War II 4 Days Prior to Dec. 7" contains an earlier absorbing summary of the *Lanikai* story.

[9]The use of ships of the U.S. Navy to protect convoys of merchant vessels carrying war and other supplies to England in September, October and November of 1941 offered the most obvious avenue of entry in the war for the Roosevelt war party. An extremely confused and obscurantist way of presenting what happened during this period provided a screen behind which an excuse could have been given the U.S. populace why entry into the war against England's (and now Soviet Russia's) enemy Germany was necessary. Three of these vessels, the U.S. destroyers *Greer*, *Kearny* and *Reuben James*, were hit by torpedoes from German submarines which stalked these convoys in the open ocean, and the latter of the three was sunk off the coast of Iceland with a loss of 100 officers and men. Why Roosevelt failed to use this incident as grounds for a war declaration mystified most observers, and left his belligerent supporters very unhappy with him. But somehow or other he botched every one of these affairs.

To be sure, not many of the general public were fooled as to where these ships were operating and how they became engaged in fighting with the German submarine fleet. Nor was there any real effort made to conceal what was going on. The day after the sinking of the *Reuben James*, the Associated Press released a story built around a letter written some time before by one of its crew, James Walton Rogers, to his father in Chattanooga, Tennessee which flatly revealed what they had been doing, and how long they had been doing it:

> We saw and contacted several subs on this 37-day cruise. Our job is to drop ash cans [depth charges] to keep 'em scared away from the convoy, but we're asking for it.

Seaman Rogers was an astute forecaster; the *Reuben James* "got it." His letter reproduced in the AP story was front-paged in the Colorado Springs *Gazette* for November 1, 1941. Still another letter from a *Reuben James* crewman to his parents was given wide publicity by American papers the very day of the sinking. United Press disclosed the contents of a letter dated October 11 by Gene Guy Evans to his home at Vero Beach, Fla., which declared in part, "We are convoying British supply ships and it looks like we will be having a hot time pretty soon." UP dispatch in Colorado Springs *Evening Telegraph*, October 31, 1941, p.2. In view of the touchiness of this assignment of American naval vessels to the support of a belligerent, it is strange that such revealing messages were allowed to go out from involved sailors to their homes with no apparent deletions by shipboard censors. The best treatment of the intrigues in the Atlantic Ocean in the fall of 1941 is Chapter 5 of Beard's *President Roosevelt*, pp. 133-155.

[10]Caldwell, Idaho: Caxton Printers, Chapter 7, pp. 407-482.

[11]New York: Random House, 1967.

[12]In one of his syndicated columns in 1964, John Chamberlain wrote: "in 1944, the Republicans knew practically all the details about the surprise at Pearl Harbor yet were loath to put the issue into the campaign lest they reveal to the Japanese that the U.S. had broken a critical code. This columnist vividly recalls riding in a car from Elmira to Geneva, N.Y., in August of 1945 with [Gov. Thomas E.] Dewey and listening to his rueful account of the decision to say nothing about Pearl Harbor. The worst of it, from Dewey's standpoint, is that he had a suspicion that the Japanese had changed their codes long before 1944, which would have made campaign revelations about Pearl Harbor harmless to the U.S. from a military standpoint. When I talked to Tom Dewey in 1945 he thought he might have been cheated out of a winning issue in 1944."

[13]This is especially true of the most recent effort to salvage the Roosevelt administration, absolve it of any significant responsibility, and to transfer it to various figures in the Pearl Harbor defense and armed forces complex, *Pearl Harbor: Warning and Decision* (Stanford, Calif.: Stanford University Press, 1962), by Roberta Wohlstetter, in essence a very sophisticated return to the Roberts Commission ploy. There is a masterly dissection of this thesis by Lieut. Commander (ret.) Charles C. Hiles, "Roberta Wohlstetter's *Pearl Harbor: Warning and Decision*: A Candid Appraisal," in *Rampart Journal*, Winter, 1966, pp. 82-95, which is preceded by an incisive introduction by Barnes. The most humiliating analysis of Mrs. Wohlstetter's book is that by Greaves in the *National Review* (December 13, 1966, pp. 1268-1269), wherein he commented on some of the more than one hundred factual errors it contains (Admiral Morison hailed it as the "best book by far on the question of why we were

surprised at Pearl Harbor), and pointed out that the author never learned the Navy's time system as applied on its messages and documents. Mrs. Wohlstetter showed no evidence of realizing that the Navy employed Greenwich civil time, not Washington time, in the headings of its messages, and therefore the pinpoint timing which is crucial to her entire account is entirely wrong. As Greaves concludes, "How valuable is a book on pre-attack intelligence that is *five hours off* on the timing of all Naval communications coming out of Washington?" (Emphasis supplied.) And in a telling riposte to Morison, Greaves added, "How dependable is a Naval historian who acclaims such a book the best on the subject?"

[14]The full text of Hull's note to the Japanese, the so-called 'ultimatum,' demanding that the Japanese withdraw unconditionally from China and recognize the Chiang Kai-shek government, was not made public until after the Pearl Harbor attack. But its ominous import was fully recognized at the time it was delivered. David Lawrence, in his column for January 31, 1942 (published *e.g.* in the Colorado Springs *Sunday Gazette Telegraph*, February 1, 1942, p. 4), charged that this policy of suppression "deprived the American Army and Navy officers of information which would have impressed upon them the necessity for being on the alert during the 11 days that elapsed between November 26 and December 7." Lawrence went on to say, "Anybody familiar with Far Eastern affairs must have known that such a demand as America made on November 26 would make the Japanese angry . . . that Japan was smarting under the American note cannot be doubted from the following language of the reply: 'The proposal in question [that Japan withdraw from China and recognize the Chungking government] ignores Japan's sacrifices in the four years of the China affair, menaces the Empire's existence and disparages its honor and prestige.' "

[15]Commander Hiles's lengthy manuscript on the Merle-Smith Message remains unpublished. The Administration's secrecy on Rainbow 5 was breached on December 4 by the Chicago *Tribune*, which learned from a source which has never been revealed the substance of the agreement to take the country into war in the Far East without an attack on Americans first. A furious search for the source of this leak was conducted in Washington but nothing definite ever turned up, though it is now believed that someone in General Arnold's office made it available to Senator Burton K. Wheeler, one of Roosevelt's most implacable adversaries, who in turn showed it to the *Tribune*'s Washington correspondent.

[16]Full text of Sec. Knox's address in New York *Times*, December 20, 1941, pp. 1, 5-8. Knox's declaration was obviously at odds with the official apologists of the Administration of which he was a part. It has been the tireless reiteration of the latter for 35 years that such a 'warning' was sent, or indirectly learned by those on the scene prior to the attack. The genius of their approach has been concentrated on keeping the investigation of Pearl Harbor in Hawaii; the more the scene is transferred to Washington and the total situation is examined, the worse the defense of the Administration fares. See Note 18.

[17](New York: McGraw-Hill, 1963.) The essentials of Prange's book appeared in the summary in the *Reader's Digest* for October, 1963, pp. 251-299 and November, 1963, pp. 274-324.

[18]United Press report, Colorado Springs *Evening Telegram*, December 17, 1941, p. 1, for summary of above, and declaration the investigation by the board headed by Justice Roberts was frankly aimed at delaying an independent Congressional effort along similar lines.

One of the curious recent products of belated testimony bearing upon the 'warnings' aspect of the Pearl Harbor attack is that of the late John A. Burns, three times Governor of Hawaii, who, in a tape recording made in 1975 which is now part of an oral history collection in the University of Hawaii, related that he was told by Honolulu FBI chief Robert L. Shivers on or about December 1, 1941 that Hawaii would be attacked by the coming weekend. How Burns, at that time an obscure captain in the Honolulu police department, could know of this, but the military and navy commanders could not, is never explained. Burns expressed the belief that Shivers, who was among those testifying before the Roberts Commission on December 18, 1941, never told them of his advance knowledge of the attack, nor did he tell anyone else about how he came to possess this information. Burns thought Shivers had come upon this via some contacts in the FBI and was not supposed to have learned of it, as Shivers committed him to secrecy as well.

Another of Burns's assertions is erroneous. The military and naval authorities at Pearl Harbor did not go from an 'attack' to a 'sabotage' alert Saturday, December 6, as he says. General Short received instructions from his superiors in Washington to go on a 'sabotage' alert on November 27, to which he responded that same day, with a wire to Washington, which said "Have alerted for sabotage—liaison with the Navy." This message was received in Washington and initialed by both the Secretary of War and the Chief of Staff. There was never a counter-order of this sent to General Short, and Pearl Harbor remained on a 'sabotage alert' from that moment until the minute of the attack on the 7th; there never was an 'attack alert' in effect prior to the Japanese bombing. (Part of the problem here was due to Gov. Burns being terminally ill at the time of the interview, which was obviously handled by people who knew nothing about the Pearl Harbor investigations and the voluminous record growing from it.) See on this matter Barnes, *The Final Story of Pearl Harbor*, first published as the entire contents of Volume IV of the journal *Left and Right* (1968), pp. 48-69, and Greaves, "F.D.R. 's Watergate: Pearl Harbor," *Reason* (February, 1976), p. 21. The absorbing summary of the Burns taped recollections of the eve of Pearl Harbor by Peter Rosegg was published in the Honolulu *Advertiser*, October 20, 1976, pp. A-1, A-8.

[19]Lawrence syndicated column, in Colorado Springs *Evening Telegram*, September 5, 1945, p. 4.

[20]Associated Press account, Colorado Springs *Evening Telegram*, December 19, 1941, p. 1. Taft had a fairly precise understanding of the tack the Administration would follow in its search for culprits far from the seat of power, and suggested, "Perhaps the fault at Hawaii was not entirely on the admirals and generals."

[21]First quoted by Barnes in his *The Final Story of Pearl Harbor*, pp. 125-126. The original of this letter was dispatched by this writer to the University of Wyoming for placement in the Barnes papers early in 1970.

[22]Colorado Springs *Evening Telegram*, January 24, 1942, p. 1. The President hailed the Roberts Commission report as "a most painstaking and most thorough investigation and report." Its voluminous and critical shortcomings awaited the labors of subsequent official investigations and independent scholars to be laid bare.

For an insight into how far political partisanship can go in covering up the truth, one should consult the observations on the infamous way in which the Roberts Commission went about its blackening of Admiral Kimmel in the latter's own book on the entire business, *Admiral Kimmel's Story* (Chicago: Regnery, 1954), pp. 146-185.

[23]The propaganda of the Western colonial powers against Japan was ingenious. The core of it concerned the 'menace' of a 'strong' Japan, reiterated in many ways, and calculated to arouse all of Japan's Asian neighbors, in particular. That the former would have preferred a 'weak' Japan was obvious, the weaker the better. Given the debility demonstrated by nearly every other country in East Asia, Japan could have become another British India, Burma, Malaya or Ceylon, another French Indo-China, another Russian Outer Mongolia, another Dutch East Indies or another American Philippines, occupied by several Western countries, like China, or cut in two and its northern half absorbed by the Czar (or later, by the Soviets.)

The intricate and complicated economic warfare increasingly waged against Japan in lieu of the out-of-the-question physical occupation was behind the build-up of the intense pressures which culminated in Pearl Harbor and the decision of Japan to take on all the major Western colonial powers at the same time, a hopeless long-range task but one which was thought preferable to starvation into a colonial state; Japan satisfied the famous definition of a vicious animal; one which defended itself when attacked.

The occidental world invented the theory and rhetoric of free enterprise, free markets and free trade. But in the 20th century, the Western national states, when faced by undesirable consequences of adhering to their own rules, took little time to improvise schemes to circumvent them. Increasingly barred from world markets by rising tariff walls and various forms of special preference and discrimination, money systems with arbitrary values and applications, Japan began to behave in the same imperial and colonial manner, to the accompaniment of some of the most transparent hypocrisy Western statecraft was capable of fabricating. But few Japanese were intimidated by the hot air balloons launched from the Western colonial and imperial power seat in their club in the League of Nations. The British, with their Commonwealth preference system and sterling bloc, the French Empire, with a very similar but much less publicized closed system (see William S. Culbertson, *Reciprocity: A National Policy for Foreign Trade* [New York: Whittlesey House, 1937], p. 91), the U.S.A. with its Monroe Doctrine, and the Russians, with their peculiar state capitalist innovations among their captive 'republics,' were in no position to decry or ridicule the Japanese for trying to make out of the Far East an environment in which *their* security would be enhanced. Matsuoka's jibe, that after the Western powers had taught the Japanese to play colonial poker, they wanted to declare the game immoral after winning most of the chips, and get everybody to switch to contract bridge, was more than a satirical sally. And the hollow and unconvincing righteous handwringing about the sternness of the Japanese as administrators of Manchuria and Korea came in specially bad taste from those who could lay claim to the Opium Wars, the Sepoy and Tai Ping Rebellions, the Amritsar Massacre, the Boer War, the Belgian record in the Congo, the Philippine Insurrection, and several score of other Western colonial achievements the latter preferred to forget (who could not remember Churchill's gloating over the atrocities inflicted in the Northwest Territories which stand out in his *A Roving Commission?)*

An aspect of the Pacific crisis which is systematically neglected by the fuglemen of Anglo-American innocence is the increasing economic warfare carried on against the Japanese after the Roosevelt-Churchill meeting off Newfoundland in August, 1941. On October 23, the US Commerce Department reported that Japanese raw material shortages had become so acute as a result of stepped-up curtailment that Japanese trade with a number of its biggest customers had virtually stopped, and that shipping and trade with the US, the British Empire and the Netherlands East Indies had become almost "nonexistent." New York *Times,* October 24, 1941, p. 36. On December 1, the National Industrial Conference Board published a work titled "The Effects of the Allied Economic Blockade on Japan," in which it stated that normal Japanese imports of raw materials covering not only war supplies but necessities for the civilian population had been reduced about 75%, and cited a report of the Chinese News Service that the country was "on the verge of economic collapse." New York *Times,* December 2, 1941, p. 6. And in the *Congressional Record,* 77th Congress, Second Session, December 8, 1942, Rep. Jeannette Rankin, of Montana, declared that on about the same day as the NICB report on Japanese economic desperation was published, a "prominent non-Japanese oriental" had told her that the situation in the Pacific was not only "serious," but that "Japan has no choice but to go to war or to submit to economic slavery for the rest of her existence."

One peculiarity in the propaganda presentation of the Japanese to Americans is the unusual transformation which took place among them after they had been defeated and reduced to an American satellite in the era of the Truman and Eisenhower administrations and the pro-consulship of Gen. MacArthur; one would hardly have recognized what appeared in the communications media in the two decades after World War II when compared with what Americans were induced to believe in the two decades before. It appeared that the movies, radio, television and print were dealing with two utterly different races. But the first five years of the post-1945 transition period incorporated an indulgence in pretensions of righteousness, probably overcompensation for the guilt feelings felt by some over the atom bombing of Hiroshima and Nagasaki. (The famed Chinese philosopher Lin Yu-tang once observed, "It is the law of human nature that those whom we injure must be condemned.")

Of course, the whimpering eclipse of the European and American colonial system of the 19th century sort, the sudden appearance on the Asian horizon of Communism on a threatened planetary scale and the involvement of the U.S.A. and its few friends (despite the vainglorious palaver of the United Nations) in a major war with this Communism in Korea, had something to do with it. So did the breakdown of the old economic exclusion of Japan, and the opening especially of the American market to its exports, have much to do with the softening of the miseries of defeat among the Japanese, fueling a surge of new prosperity which rapidly reduced the desperation of the 1930s to a dim memory among most.

In retrospect the literature which taught Americans that the Japanese were a backward and primitive people who could be scattered by a show of force in a few days and who had nothing to offer the world of consequence is curious and pathetic in its horrendous misconceptions. A land which was not supposed to be able to conduct a war longer than a few weeks against Western powers, according to a long string of our most mighty political and military pundits, turned out to be a shock of major proportions. If Japanese industry could not penetrate the Anglo-American tariff barriers with more than cheap electric light bulbs, ten-cent-store toys and flimsy Christmas tree ornaments, it was able to demonstrate to the British a superior aerial torpedo when Japanese naval flyers sank the *Repulse* and the *Prince of Wales* in less than a quarter of an hour, and a superior combat fighter airplane in the Zero to American forces in the Pacific War. One can search works from Freda Utley's *Japan's Feet of Clay* to Ambassador Joseph C. Grew's *Ten Years in Japan* and learn precious little of pre-Pearl Harbor Japan. In fact, there is virtually nothing on Japan worth reading produced between the World Wars other than John Patric's *Yankee Hobo in the Orient.*

What the various communists, socialists, liberals, conservatives, Old China Hands, 19th century imperialists and colonialists said should be done about Japan between 1919 and 1939 filled libraries, and it was generally wrong. What Lawrence Dennis once described as "the bloody futility of frustrating the strong" was never more dramatically demonstrated than in the attempt to save the 18th and 19th centuries in the Far East between 1931 and 1945.

The Framing of
'TOKYO ROSE'

Iva Toguri 1945

THE FRAMING OF 'TOKYO ROSE'

It is a very comfortable feeling to imagine that there is no past and that the future begins with the present but the future has a very awkward way of reminding us that our past will not down.
—Francis Neilson, in *The American Journal of Economics and Sociology* (July, 1949), p.358.

World War Two ended over thirty years ago, but the unfinished business of this war clutters the planet. Big political questions involving unresolved territorial disposition of disputed regions have brought about the vicious Korean and Vietnam wars. The nearly thirty years of strife in the Mideast grows out of other aspects of unbalanced WW 2 accounts. The boundaries and structure of Germany are still as unsettled as they were three decades ago, and "war crimes" trials still go on there.[2] For that matter, there still is no general peace treaty ending the war of 1939-1945.

On another level, there are many incidents which appear to be settled permanently, but which are really in a kind of historical limbo, with the final word, if there ever will be one, far from forthcoming. One of these, the subject of this re-appraisal, is the infamous treason trial of the woman known around the world three decades ago as 'Tokyo Rose,' and which, despite accepted modern legendry, has never been resolved. We already have a generation which has only the haziest notions as to what this case was all about, if they have any understanding about it at all.[3] But very few of those old enough to recall the case realize that the person found guilty in the trial of 1949 has never admitted any guilt, and furthermore, her original attorneys sought for 25 years thereafter to establish not only that she was innocent, but that she should be pardoned and compensated for past indignities she was forced to endure.

It is desirable to start this amazing narrative on a broad scale, however, so that it can be understood how the whole sorry tale became part of the history of the times.

The attack on Pearl Harbor by the Japanese on December 7, 1941 brought the USA into World War Two formally. And Americans fought the Japanese in the Pacific for nearly four years thereafter, about twice as long as they eventually fought the Germans and Italians in Europe. It was a veritable race war (Norman Thomas once described World War II in the Pacific as "an organized race riot"), and the accompanying propaganda was pitched at a level of racial venom in the USA which many involved never did repudiate. Hatred of the Japanese was developed into a science by the war administration's propaganda arm, and on some levels it became so aggravated that one would have imagined Americans were fighting large insects in the Pacific islands, so degraded did the enemy become on the evolutionary scale invented by the clever chaps who prepared the material for the psychological warfare which was fought simultaneously against the home front. A cursory examination of the popular press of 1941-45 reveals substantial slanderous dehumanization of the enemy in Asia, but it was far worse on what might be called the vulgar or informal level.

It is not the purpose here to dwell on this aspect of the war, but it is necessary to have some understanding of the state of mind in super-heated post-war America toward the late enemy in the Far East. It was part of the emotional climate in which such trials as that of "Tokyo Rose" took place.[4] It was many years before any headway was discernible in the effort to dissipate the ferocity of Japanophobia in the USA, and overtones of this clever and successful brainwashing are palpable to this day, thanks in part to the reappearance of war-time anti-Japanese movies on television (since 1945 a very large part of American youth must reach the age of 14 or so before they realize the Germans and Japanese are no longer our enemies).

Though much balderdash had emanated from 'experts' and even military and naval spokesmen in the decade before Pearl to the effect that the Japanese could not put up a decent fight against Americans for six months, that an American fighting man was worth at least half a dozen Asiatics,[5] and that any encounter in the Pacific, predicted by all manner of 'seers' after the Russo-Japanese War of 1904-05, would be little more than an outing, it was soon realized in 1942 that the USA was confronted by a tough, resourceful and intelligent enemy. And it was also now being conceded that it was going to be a long and bitter struggle.

A steady drumfire of verbal abuse of the enemy was a substitute for victories for a time, and nothing was neglected which might be employed to paint the adversary as a monster. Beginning late in 1941 American servicemen stationed in various parts of the Pacific war theater began to receive on their radios numerous broadcasts of American music, that of the big dance bands which was at its peak of popularity with the young. These recordings were accompanied by commentary by announcers, most of whom were English-speaking women. Though there were several of them, the soldiers and sailors referred to them all as a single person, whom they dubbed "Tokyo Rose." Though no such name was ever used on Radio Tokyo, from which these broadcasts originated, it did not matter in those days.

The exploits of this legendary disc jockey grew to wondrous proportions, and her fame spread in such a way that by the war's end there were few people in the USA who had not heard of her. Mothers imagined her as a purring, leering Lorelei who was undermining their cleancut sons with all manner of unmentionable suggestions and especially encouraging them to believe wives and girl friends at home were "untrue," among other things. The press boiled with stories about this omnipresent woman, and radio blatherskites such as Walter Winchell[6] and Drew Pearson were much exercised over it all.

With this brief background in mind, we may begin properly the *historia calamitatum* of Iva Ikuko Toguri. Born on July 4, 1916 of Japanese parents in Los Angeles, she graduated from UCLA in 1940. She was an outstanding pre-medical student there, as well as a talented pianist. The pre-war decade being a time of poor opportunities for Nisei in the US, she thought for a time of going to Japan to study medicine. But when she did go, in 1941, she went at the request of her parents to visit an ailing aunt in Kyushu; Iva's mother was too ill to undertake the visit herself.[7]

And it was while she was there at the home of her uncle that the Pearl Harbor attack took place, from which time her life became incredibly complicated. She later related the confusion that took place caused by her inability to speak Japanese, and her unwillingness to believe at the start that such a thing had actually happened. It was two days after Pearl that she knew for sure that war had broken out.[8]

That she was still in Japan on December 7, 1941 was principally the fault of incompetent bureaucrats of two countries. She had left Los Angeles in such a hurry that she did not wait to obtain a passport, and was supplied only with what was called a "certificate of identification." When she tried to sail home on the *Tatsu Maru* in November, 1941, the failure of the US consul to have her passport ready and the inability of the Japanese monetary functionaries to expedite the exchange of her foreign funds caused her to miss the ship.

She tried to get back to the USA two more times by sea on the Swedish ship *Gripsholm*, which was engaged much of the early war on runs from one belligerent to another, carrying refugees back and forth. The first time was just before the war; she failed again in September, 1942. By the latter date her parents were locked up in Arizona's Gila River concentration camp (this and like camps are still described in that exquisite hypocrisy Americans have inherited from their English tradition as 'relocation centers'[9]) and she was unable to get the money for the passage from them under these circumstances. Her mother later died in one of these camps.

But the troubles of Iva Toguri were just beginning. Her money soon ran out, and she became increasingly an object of suspicion, badgered by the Japanese police, who could not understand why she did not renounce her US citizenship. Matters were made worse by the breakdown in communication. She was denied a ration card, disowned by her uncle, and ended up wandering the streets of Tokyo for three months, following which she was admitted to a hospital, suffering from malnutrition.[10]

Then began the job of survival in a strange land, with which her own country was at war, as unfavorable a situation as one was likely to imagine. First she set out to learn some Japanese. Then she secured a job with the Domei News Agency (Japan's equivalent to the big national news-gathering enterprises such as Reuter's, Havas and many others), but apparently was too pro-American for her associates. She soon left here, taking part-time work as a typist with the Danish Legation and Radio Tokyo. This latter place turned out to be a fateful one. Here she came to the attention of an Australian prisoner of war, Major Charles E. Cousens. Cousens, an American of similar status, Major Wallace G. Ince, and

Norman Reyes, a lieutenant in the Filipino army, were in charge of a POW-oriented radio program over Radio Tokyo, which became popularly known under the title Zero Hour.[11] It was broadcast mainly by English-speaking women announcers, who accompanied programs of American dance band music with casual chit-chat, virtually devoid of politics or propaganda, though there were other women who did read news and commentary on the war on several different programs.[12] There was in the Zero Hour scripts, prepared under the direction of and mostly by the above-mentioned men, a theme which vaguely accented home and the comforts of non-combatant life, which could be and was construed as an effort to undermine the morale of Americans fighting a long distance from home in a very strange environment. It was originally the backbone of the Government's case against Iva Toguri that she had broadcast this kind of material, not that she had made political propaganda in behalf of Imperial Japan, though it might be mentioned that in a 1968 Pennsylvania State University Speech Department thesis by Rose Maria Fazio, which sought to estimate the effects of these broadcasts during the war, 93% of the ex-servicemen who were sent questionnaires responded that hearing these broadcasts had no demoralizing effect on them.[13]   Iva Toguri encountered Major Cousens for the first time in November, 1943, nearly two full years after Allied soldiers in the Pacific had started calling Radio Tokyo women announcers 'Tokyo Rose.'[14] Cousens declared he selected her because she had demonstrated sympathy with POWs, and had secretly obtained food, clothing and blankets for them. She was coached and helped on a voice test, and soon joined the team of women on the air with Zero Hour.[15]

The events of the period of her employment are not clear,[16] and were made much muddier by the continuous contradictions voiced by a stream of witnesses during the 1949 trial. Some of this will be examined in the context of the trial. At this moment we can proceed to the end of the war and reconstruct the time span from the late summer of 1945 to the spring of 1949.

The fierce search for 'Tokyo Rose' on the part of American journalists coincided with two other developments also transpiring in the closing days of August and the early days of September, 1945. The first of these was the steady pouring into the Tokyo area of large numbers of American occupying troops. Their mood was one of grimness verging on to vindictiveness, an attitude liberally stoked by a plethora of atrocity stories. The latter came from all regions which had housed prisoners of war in particular, and their tempo and gravity increased with almost every passing hour. The newspapers in the USA bulged with an avalanche of these accounts in this same time, the high point of which probably was the release of an official report by the Australian government on September 10, which accused the Japanese forces of cannibalism.[17] When the big Tokyo newspaper *Asahi* asserted that part of the motivation for the multitude of atrocity stories which were filling many columns in the stateside newspapers was a coverup for US atrocities against the Japanese, the paper was suspended for two days by General Douglas MacArthur, who had replaced Emperor Hirohito as Japan's authority figure.[18]

Thus the effort to locate 'Tokyo Rose' was no mere quest for a good headline; it was colored by a spirit of maliciousness which reflected the general tenor of the occupation, and there would obviously be little time spent considering the niceties of accuracy, considerateness or any of the other virtues of a less hysterical and more civilized psychological climate. Clark Lee and Harry T. Brundidge were anything but alone in the journalistic hunt for 'Tokyo Rose.' Al Dopking, of Lee's previous employer, the Associated Press, published a lengthy story on September 1 on his feverish quest for this elusive figure. He spoke of being conducted through Yokohama by an American-born Japanese girl who had come to Japan from Downey, California in 1940, and had worked at Domei for two years during the war. He reported that she had told him 'Tokyo Rose' was "several girls" and that she knew three of them herself, two of them Los Angeles-born, who worked at Radio Tokyo. Despite his eager pursuit, Dopking half-despaired of success, and was almost reconciled to believing that the woman-starved Pacific theater servicemen had been gulled by a Japanese propaganda invention all along. [19]

But at the very moment Dopking's account was being read, one of the suspected materializations of 'Tokyo Rose,' Iva Toguri, was being interviewed by rival journalists Lee and Brundidge in the Imperial Hotel in Tokyo. The interview was to lead to a swatch of notes hurriedly composed by Lee, in which he managed among other things both to pose questions to his interviewee and answer them as well, with the result that a subsequently published account of the interview by Lee included self-damning remarks attributed to Iva Toguri which she never uttered. More attention will be paid to the central part played by this famous pair of interrogators subsequently but it was the refusal of Brundidge's employer, *Cosmopolitan* magazine, to print his sensational account of the affair that led to her arrest as 'Tokyo Rose.' [20]

Part of the blame has to be assessed against Iva Toguri as well, as a consequence of her rather naive and innocent approach to the interview, which in large part grew from her conviction that she had done nothing wrong, and her belief that the reporters were trying to verify the truth, rather than to weave a web of sinister circumstance around her which could lead only to implacable pursuit as a traitor. Fingered by Brundidge at U.S. Eighth Army intelligence headquarters she was arrested and placed under detention on September 5, 1945. [21]

American military occupation and civil agencies then began a curious game with the defendant. Released the day after her first arrest, news about her began to proliferate at home, and a week later it was revealed that a United States Attorney sought to have her tried in the United States. [22]

On October 17, 1945 she was arrested again, and after spending a month in a Yokohama prison, was transferred to the ominous Sugamo prison in Tokyo, where the principal Japanese accused of war crimes were jailed. Here she was to stay for the next eleven months. [23]

The occupation authorities decided as early as April, 1946 that she had done nothing culpable under military law, and privately decided to abandon any prosecution, and gave her unconditional clearance of treason charges.[24] But as a result of a separate Department of Justice investigation she remained in jail. In September the Department gradually adopted the view that they should desist from prosecuting her and an Assistant Attorney General recommended to Washington that the Government drop the case, which was done on October 21,[25] and on October 25, 1946, Iva Toguri was released from jail. The government's contention was re-affirmed that the appellation 'Tokyo Rose' was a composite one, and that it was impossible to isolate any individual under such a designation.[26]

During this year in prison she was never allowed legal counsel, never knew the charges against her, nor granted either bail or the constitutionally-prescribed 'speedy trial.' At one time held *incommunicado*, her husband was eventually allowed to visit her for a grand total of *twenty minutes a month*. In the meantime she was treated as a circus freak, subjected to involuntary visits from all manner of people, even American congressmen, and even while she was bathing, in order that various gawking bumpkins might have a glimpse of the woman alleged to be the notorious 'Tokyo Rose.'

The Tokyo Rose saga might very well have ended here had it not been for an apparently unrelated circumstance, and its complicated consequences. On April 19, 1945 Iva Toguri had married a fellow media worker, Felipe J. D'Aquino, of mixed Portuguese and Japanese extraction, and technically a Portuguese citizen. When she became pregnant in 1947, the year after her release from prison, and thinking it would be appropriate to have her child born in the United States, she applied for a passport.

Now began a torturous process of legal shillyshallying as to her citizenship status. When jailed in the fall of 1945 one of the first things which had been established and promoted via the press was her United States citizenship.[27] Now the complications of other bureaucratic bungling set in. She had been cleared by the Army and Justice Department, and the latter in October, 1947 had 'no objection' to the State department issuing her a passport.

The release of the news of her application to the press soon had the sensation mongers in full cry, and her exploitation for headlines had much to do with her new round of dolors. But there were many contributors to this. It ran from the mischievous sensation seekers Lee and Brundidge to radio bawlers such as Walter Winchell,[28] the latter spearheading a ferocious hostility.[29] Eventually it spread to the American Legion, and to such as the Native Sons and Daughters of the Golden West, and about every other pocket of professional Japanophobia still awash in the wake of World War Two.[30] The various outcries against the return of a native born American to her native land performed the function of a delaying action, and Iva Toguri D'Aquino's baby was stillborn in January, 1948.

Between October and December, 1947 some amazing and powerful pressure was applied to the Truman regime's Justice Department to re-open the 'Tokyo Rose' charges against Iva Toguri D'Aquino. Preparations began to invest considerable time and money in this inquisition, which when directed against suspected Stalinist spies and agents was usually decried with much emotion by liberals as a 'witch hunt.' And it apparently made no difference to the new (and old) stalkers that both the Army and Justice investigations in Japan had been concluded in her favor.

On December 3, 1947 the FBI announced that it was once more seeking witnesses in a projected re-opening of the treason charges.[31] The most enthusiastic respondent was Brundidge, now identified as "an ex-Hearst reporter." No doubt smarting from Winchell's pointed attack on the air as a maladroit, he undertook to ingratiate himself with J. Edgar Hoover, offering to assist the FBI in searching out witnesses against Mrs. D'Aquino in Japan, as well as trying to get her to sign the Lee notes of 1945, in order to clinch the allegations he and Lee had been making ever since the celebrated interview in Tokyo in September, 1945, that they had a 'confession' from her.

In March, 1948 Brundidge accompanied U.S. Attorney John B. Hogan on a trip to Japan. On the 26th, Hogan and Brundidge interviewed Mrs. D'Aquino again, and Hogan noted to a superior that she had declined to sign the notes proffered once more by Brundidge, on the grounds that they contained numerous and obvious discordances and incongruities between the story she had told the reporters and what these notes now contained.[32]

Brundidge then found for Atty. Hogan and the Justice Department two Japanese who were willing to testify that they had witnessed Mrs. D'Aquino making treasonable broadcasts during the war: Hiromu Yagi, a Japan Travel Bureau agent, and Toshikatsu Kodairi, an Associated Press reporter in Japan.[33] So the way now seemed clear to proceed in calling a grand jury to 'sift' the treason charges against Mrs. D'Aquino, as the New York *Times* put it.

From here on, the trying of Iva Toguri D'Aquino in the newspapers and via opinion generated by radio bawlers was to proceed for over a year prior to her actual legal proceedings, which should have had professional liberal civil rights watchdogs baying around the clock. But these vigilant protectors of the legal prerogatives of hardened criminals, Communists and related ideologues were strangely silent. Nor were their legions of journalist allies any more watchful of the sacred civil rights and constitutional liberties of a fellow American-born citizen, who was still unproven of having done anything to anyone anywhere.

By mid-August, 1948 Mrs. D'Aquino was front page news again. The *Times* featured her interview on the 16th and devoted an editorial to her two days later. On the 26th she was arrested and imprisoned in Tokyo once more, and plans were set for her return to the United States the next day. But statements on the circumstances of her return and to what part of the USA consisted of a torturous medley of contradictions.

Since the accused was alleged to have committed treason abroad, the law stipulated that trials for such offenses had to take place at the first point on American soil where the accused set foot. The ship bringing her to the USA pointedly skipped docking in Hawaii and proceeded directly to San Francisco, avoiding a location where she might have been the recipient of very tolerant treatment in the courts, and taking her instead to a mainland city where the reputation for Japanophobia was substantial.

Mrs. D'Aquino was arraigned before a federal commissioner on September 25 and lodged in a jail near Chinatown. So she was finally back home, even if a prisoner once more, a state of affairs which now surely was becoming familiar.[34]

Segments of the opulent establishment press convicted her nearly a year before her trial began. The scurrilous lead national affairs article in *Time* on August 30, 1948[35] flatly called her a "traitor," scoffed at her story of why she went to Japan in 1941, while implying that her treasonous motivation antedated the war. But this vicious attack concealed as "news" admitted that she had been just one of more than a half dozen English-speaking Japanese girls on Radio Tokyo, and that there was no evidence that American servicemen had been disturbed by the 'Tokyo Rose' broadcasts (a poll of veterans in 1948 might have revealed that 'Tokyo Rose,' *in toto*, had far more admirers among their ranks than detractors.)

Some sectors of the American press devoted to the welfare of Alger Hiss used the re-opening of the 'Tokyo Rose' case as a welcome relief and diversion from their chores involved in defense of the former, whose investigation before Congress was at a full peak at that moment. Many socially and financially prominent super-liberals were undergoing bloody sweats in behalf of Hiss, probably their most dearly loved pet protege in this century. A penniless and nearly friendless girl of Japanese ancestry made an easy punching bag.[36]

Under the impact of such trashy bus station and supermarket 'literary' gossip-mongering and exacerbation of wartime hatreds was the whole sorry process of 'Tokyo Rose' again dragged across the nation's consciousness. The combination of the Brundidge-Lee and Winchell effusions (plus that of Kate Smith), in addition to Brundidge's 'cooperation' with the Justice Department, led to the re-opening of the case by Attorney General Tom C. Clark, father of Ramsey Clark, of recent Hanoi fame. (It was Atty. Gen. Clark who ordered her re-arrest but Brundidge took personal credit for Atty. Gen. Clark's order to the U.S. Army occupiers in Tokyo and her transport to San Francisco.)

A federal grand jury indictment for treason on October 8, 1948,[37] during which irregularities took place that should have caused its dismissal, as shall be seen, led to a decision to prosecute on the part of the Government. Iva Toguri D'Aquino was front page news again.

An examination of the grand jury proceedings which led to the indictment of Iva Toguri D'Aquino on eight counts of treason certainly leads to no conclusion that the Government should be covered with glory. The U.S. Attorney responsible for conducting the Government's case before the grand jury was Thomas De Wolfe; he later was to head the prosecution when the trial began. De Wolfe, however, five months before the grand jury began its hearings, expressed strong views to the effect that there were insufficient grounds and evidence which would lead to her conviction. He thought the witnesses would present overwhelming evidence as to her pro-American and non-treasonous behavior while employed by Radio Tokyo, that there was no available evidence which might induce 'reasonable' minds to 'conclude guilt beyond a reasonable doubt,' and that on the basis of where they stood at that moment, 'the Government case must fail.'

[42]

De Wolfe must have been inspired by what Hogan and Brundidge brought back from Japan, however, since he undertook the presentation of the Government's case with un-ordinary vigor in October. He boasted of presenting the evidence against Mrs. D'Aquino 'in a rather forceful manner,' in a memorandum written November 12, 1948, and in another composed on November 17 he admitted that even after this bravura performance, two grand jurors were still voting against indictment, and that he found it necessary 'to practically make a Fourth of July speech in order to obtain an indictment.'

But within less than a month of the grand jury indictment, there must have been prostration among the men preparing the prosecution, because by then they knew that both of the Japanese witnesses against the defendant, Yagi, and Kodaira, had perjured themselves. Yagi had testified that Kodaira had been present with him at the time of a Zero Hour broadcast where they had heard the defendant make treasonous remarks. Yagi confessed before a Counter-Intelligence officer in November in Japan that this was not so, and on November 5, Kodaira emphatically denied ever having been present with Yagi at any such broadcast, implicating Brundidge as having cajoled him to so attest, and promising vague benefits in the United States if he would so testify.

At first the grand jury refused to act unless the officers under whom Mrs. D'Aquino had worked, and had read from scripts they had written, were also indicted. They settled for only the single indictment when informed that they had no authority over military officers; the latter could only be court martialed. (Cousens, tried in Australia, was acquitted of treason charges and promoted. In the US, Ince was similarly promoted, and, as Phil Jordan, one of the most knowledgeable students of the case, observes tartly, "with no nonsense about a court martial," though the Government had promised the grand jury that this would take place in return for their cooperation in finding against Mrs. D'Aquino.)

First scheduled for May 16, 1949[38] in Federal Court in San Francisco, the trial did not get under way until July 5, Judge Michael J. Roche presiding. The jury consisted of six men and six women, all white Californians, selected in just two hours. Stanton Delaplane, covering the event for the San Francisco *Chronicle*, in the issue for July 5 called special attention to the prosecution eliminating all non-Caucasian potential jurors, employing eight of its peremptory challenges to eliminate six blacks, a Chinese-American and another person of mixed ethnic origins.[39] But others paid close scrutiny to this unusual Government tactic, and during the trial and long after there were charges of intentional racism, which were heatedly denied by Government spokesmen. However, it could not be missed by many that an all-white jury was trying a Japanese-American in a state long known for its Japanophobic outrages and persisting psychology and sentiment, gravely inflamed by the recently-concluded war.[40] (It might be pointed out that the Government subsequently segregated its witnesses, the Caucasians in one room and the Japanese in another, while they awaited being called to testify.)

[43]

The prosecution was headed by De Wolfe (see above), special assistant to Atty. Gen. Clark, assisted by two U.S. attorneys, Frank J. Hennessey and Hogan, Brundidge's companion on the witness-hunting trip to Japan. De Wolfe was a specialist in treason trials, having already acted in the successful prosecution of American journalists Robert H. Best and Douglas Chandler, convicted for making wartime broadcasts from Germany.

Defense counsel was headed by Wayne M. Collins, aided by Theodore Tamba and George Olshausen, San Francisco attorneys, who served the defendant without pay. The performance of Collins in particular caused the prosecution many unhappy and uneasy days, achieving such success in cross-examination of prosecution witnesses that there were few observers who believed the Government had a case by the time it went to the jury.

By the time the trial began, Mrs. D'Aquino, following her arrest in Tokyo August 25, 1948 and her transport to San Francisco and arraignment on September 25, had been in jail or its equivalent another year. (There is an unfortunate NEA telephoto published in the daily newspapers all over the land in the days after the start of the trial of Mrs. D'Aquino being escorted into the courtroom by a Government policeman under appearances which suggest she is almost being dragged, though it would seem that it was due to being shot at a bad angle; however, the malicious may have preferred to view it on the obvious superficial merits.)

Some poorly-explained things transpired before and during the 'Tokyo Rose' trial. Three and a half months before the trial the court had denied a defense motion to subpoena 34 witnesses in Japan, including even General Douglas MacArthur, the veritable American pro-consul, whose prestige and status rivalled anything ever achieved by Caesar in the Roman Empire.[41] The court allowed the collection of depositions from witnesses in Japan by the defense, but the posting of pieces of paper, no matter what they contained, could never match in drama and effect a live witness, no matter how informational the deposition, and no matter how dull, obtuse or mendacious the witness. The Government, on the other hand, utilized witnesses brought in from Germany and Japan, including 19 Japanese citizens flown in first class from Tokyo at a cost of $23,000, and who were paid $10 a day for the duration of the trial, which exceeded 12 weeks. It was the testimony of two of these Japanese nationals, unsupported by an American citizen, which led to the conviction of Mrs. D'Aquino on a single count of treason.

Ultimately the Government, which rejected defense efforts to bring in witnesses from Japan, on the grounds that it did not have the money to pay for this, spared little expense in its own behalf, spending upward of three fourths of a million dollars to send Iva Toguri D'Aquino to jail, and undoubtedly going well beyond the million mark in keeping her in jail for 74 months and in paying for the multifarious bureaucratic maneuvers and capers which have been engaged in for over a quarter of a century in continuing its ferocious offensive against a solitary citizen.[42]

The defense was guilty of one serious lapse, as Atty. Tamba was to recall later, in failing to realize that Major General Charles A. Willoughby was right in San Francisco, based at the Presidio, at the time of the trial. Gen.

Willoughby was chief of intelligence for the U.S. occupation forces in Japan in 1945-46, and supervised the Defense Department investigation which had dismissed treason charges against Iva Toguri D'Aquino at that time. He might have been a formidable witness for the defense, if not the deciding factor in the trial.

The government prosecution started out anxious to prove that she had volunteered to broadcast on Radio Tokyo and that she had committed treasonous acts.[43] A former serviceman[44] witness the first day testified that he had got her autograph in 1945. But the fireworks did not commence until the second day, when Yukio Ikeda, wartime personnel director of Radio Tokyo, and Shigetsugu Tsuneishi, the military commander who directed the POW broadcasts on Zero Hour, testified for the prosecution. The latter asserted that no POWs were forced to broadcast pro-Japanese propaganda. Under cross-examination Tsuneishi expressed doubt that the "Tokyo Rose" broadcast amounted to anything effective in the propaganda field anyway, and further supported the accused by admitting she had been under duress to broadcast on the famed program.[45] This particular ploy turned out to be one which went on all during the trial. The prosecution's attempt to show that the defendant had not acted under duress, and the countering of the defense to demonstrate that she had, proved unfruitful, as the witnesses were hopelessly contradictory on that subject, and on most others as well, all during the trial.

Clark Lee, testifying July 14, following Tsuneishi, who was on the stand four days, made some headway for the prosecution, when he recounted things which allegedly had been said to him in his 1945 interview with the defendant. It was also his testimony, and that of one Leslie Nakashima, which disclosed the sinister sensationalism of the former's colleague, Brundidge. Lee and Brundidge came into Tokyo promptly on the heels of the occupying U.S. Marines, and immediately smelled a journalistic coup in the making if they could be the first to locate and interview the universally-discussed 'Tokyo Rose.'

They soon found out that there were several possible candidates here, and it was purely coincidental that they ended up with Iva Toguri D'Aquino. Seeking help from Nakashima, a Domei employe, they got none. But Nakashima then went to Radio Tokyo and consulted John Kenkichi Oki, production supervisor of the Zero Hour. Nakashima, testifying early in the first week of September, declared that Oki told him there was no such person as "Tokyo Rose," that there were several women who had been on Radio Tokyo record shows, and then for some unknown reason gave him Mrs. D'Aquino's name.

Unabashed by these complications, Lee asked Nakashima to find her for him and Brundidge, and to offer her $2000 for a story in which she would admit that she was THE 'Tokyo Rose.' He did not make clear whether she got any money,[46] but these two opportunist reporters got a five-hour interview with her, and Lee clung to his earlier declaration that she had admitted what they had tried to get her to say. Under cross-examination, Lee admitted that they had omitted from their story everything that might have been in her favor.[47]

[45]

The singular aspect of this episode was that Brundidge, who was listed as a witness by the prosecution, was never called to testify, nor was he subpoenaed by the defense as a possible hostile witness. The behavior of the prosecution is far more understandable than that of the defense, however. The Attorney General's office knew full well a month before the trial began that the defense also knew of the confessions of perjury by Yagi and Kodaira, and would cross-examine Brundidge if he took the stand as a prosecution witness. The Government had considered prosecuting Brundidge for subornation of perjury, but became convinced that any such action prior to the trial of Mrs. D'Aquino would completely wreck any hope on their part of getting her convicted. The assistant attorney general for the criminal division also was sure that he would never be convicted in California on the testimony of two Japanese, and that they had better forget for the present any idea of instituting criminal proceedings against him.

The most damaging witnesses against Mrs. D'Aquino, however, proved to be Oki, and his associate, George Mitsushio, chief of the "Front Line" section of Radio Tokyo which produced Zero Hour. Testifying during the third week of July, both men stubbornly stuck to a declaration that they had seen or heard her broadcasting the false news report concerning the alleged American naval losses in the Leyte Gulf battle in October, 1944, of which more will be said later. This was no. VI of the eight-part indictment, the only one on which she was convicted.

These two witnesses deserve extra attention. Oki, born in Sacramento, had played football at New York University, and was married to one of the girl broadcasters on Radio Tokyo, known during the war as the "Saturday night party girl." Mitsushio, born in San Francisco, had gone to Japan in the years before the war, like Oki, and subsequently both renounced their U.S. citizenship.[48] It was an additional touch of irony that it was to be their testimony that brought about the conviction of a Japanese-American who did *not* renounce her U.S. citizenship.

Undoubtedly both were under tremendous pressure to testify the way the prosecution wished, and were surely subject at least to psychic intimidation by FBI investigators, since they could have been rung in on a treason charge themselves through a little expert rigging. Their dogged maintenance that the fateful newscast had been uttered by the defendant made defense counsel suspicious. Collins pounded Mitsushio especially, drawing an admission that the latter had memorized the indictment. At one time he supported 7 of the 8 counts thereon, but ultimately fell back on No. VI, which position he did not desert.

Mitsushio's mechanical repetition of the legalese of the indictment led to additional questioning from Collins, and eventually drew from him the admission that he had received a copy from the prosecutor, De Wolfe, two weeks before testifying, and that he had kept it until three days before taking the stand. Both men further undermined their credibility by giving contradictory testimony to each other as to the ultimate purpose of the Zero Hour program, on which subject they were the experts.[49] But the damage had been done.

The performance of Mitsushio in particular smacked of witness-preparation, and other performances on the stand reinforced this defense contention. Shinjiro Igarashi, a Radio Tokyo broadcaster who testified in the sixth week of the trial, had previously told two of the defense counsel on April 22, 1949 in Japan that Mrs. D'Aquino had never made any statement on the air concerning alleged American naval sinkings at Leyte Gulf. But on the stand in San Francisco he reversed his statement. When challenged on this by Collins, Igarashi replied, "At that time my memory was confused," to which Collins countered in cutting words, "And now it's much better, isn't it?" Harris Sugiyama, another prosecution witness, also admitted that his memory had been "refreshed" since he had arrived in San Francisco to testify.[50]

An interesting footnote was later added to the story of Oki and Mitsushio. Jordan, who along with retired US Army Colonel John Juji Hada are among the best informed men alive on the ramifications of the 'Tokyo Rose' affair, related that Atty. Tamba had once told him of being approached during a noon recess by a witness brought to the court from Japan, but who was never allowed to testify, one Seizu Huga. Huga told Tamba that the two men testifying to the alleged treasonable act by Mrs. D'Aquino were lying, and that if called to the stand and cross-examined, he would say so, and present evidence in support of his charge which would make the prosecution's case collapse. But Huga never made the stand; he was sent back to Japan a few hours after being seen talking to Tamba.[51]

From now on it was downhill for prosecutor De Wolfe. His witnesses tended to go from bad to worse under cross-examination by Collins, especially when the Government started calling Americans. Dale Kramer, a 1945 reporter for the service magazine *Yank*, testified that Mrs. D'Aquino did not use the name 'Tokyo Rose' (but then, neither did anyone else ever do so). He did cite a script in which she called herself "Orphan Ann" (Cousens later explained that the "Ann" was short for "announcer," and that the remainder was related to the popular song which sprang from the American comic strip syndicated in the daily newspapers. However, it had an internal meaning to the defendant, who thought of herself as an 'orphaned' American working on the radio in a strange land.)

One of the most damaging to the prosecution's case was the next one, an FBI agent named Frederick G. Tillman, who, though a prosecution witness, told the court that the defendant had told him that she construed her purpose on Zero Hour to be one of making the program entertaining while reducing its effectiveness as propaganda. He further testified under cross-examination to the frantic efforts Mrs. D'Aquino had made to try to get back to the US before the war broke out, which was contained in the 12-page statement she had made for him in Sugamo Prison on April 30, 1946, several months prior to her second release by American authorities.[53]

The bomb, however, was dropped by Tillman under cross-examination, when he admitted that Yagi, the Japan Travel Bureau agent, and a Government witness, had confessed to him that he was bribed to testify falsely against Mrs. D'Aquino before the grand jury which indicted her.[54] It seemed that this was the most important opening of the whole trial which might have been exploited by the defense, but Brundidge, the man who had bribed Yagi, was not even identified in court at the moment Tillman admitted the bribery under Atty. Collins' questioning. The failure to subpoena Brundidge on the part of the defense later on appears to have been a grave lapse. This was made more obvious when the defense early in September was unable to introduce testimony from Yagi on the bribery incident, though it did submit Kodaira's deposition from Japan on Brundidge.

The day before this damaging admission by Tillman, the prosecution had put on the stand two counter-intelligence agents, one of them Major James T. Reitz, who had been a captain in the CIC in Tokyo in September, 1945 but who had to be brought to San Francisco from his new assignment in Germany. Major Reitz identified a package of radio scripts which had been turned over to him by Sgt. Merritt Page, also of the CIC, in Tokyo. And Page, employed in 1949 with the Veterans Administration in Pittsburgh, followed Reitz to the stand and declared that the scripts had been given to him by Mrs. D'Aquino in the Grand Hotel in Tokyo, at which time Page said she had told him that she did not believe she had done anything treasonous. The proceedings here were not very supportive of the prosecution either, since it would have been strange behavior on the part of anyone believing themselves to be traitorous to volunteer the evidence upon which such a verdict might be secured, self-incrimination of the most suspicious sort. The counter-intelligence sleuths were also helping out the defense.

A third witness that same day (July 26), another former reporter for *Yank*, James J. Keeney, supported the previous testimony of his colleague Kramer, declaring that the defendant had also confirmed to Kramer, who had interviewed her in Tokyo on September 3, 1945, of the part of the Australian POW, Cousens, in getting her the job on Zero Hour. And under cross-examination by Collins, Keeney stated that Mrs. D'Aquino had denied that she ever broadcast to American servicemen that their wives and sweethearts were "going out with other men."[55] (That they had done so could have been established on a grand scale; therefore, *if* Mrs. D'Aquino had made such a statement, how she could have been considered traitorous for simply reporting a common social fact of wartime American life, is truly a mystery. But the myth of Stateside fidelity had to be protected, even though one of the most widespread and universal home front and war front jokes concerned some incident or other involving a 'Dear John letter.')

Probably the most persuasive of the defense tactics was the emphasizing that the Government was trying to prove that the defendant was each of all the women broadcasters on Radio Tokyo during World War Two, and was not interested in learning who they all were. The defense maintained Mrs. D'Aquino was a victim of mistaken identity, and being blamed for the words of others. There is no doubt that the testimony by the defendant and others, that there were several other women involved in the Zero Hour broadcasting, whom careless or malicious people had lumped together as a single person, had something to do with the change in approach by the prosecution.

Defense counsel made hash out of the prosecution's witnesses who testified to hearing Mrs. D'Aquino while stationed at widely separated geographical locations.[56] Radio Tokyo had 20 transmitters, broadcasting from Nazaki, Yamata and Kawachi in Japan, and at the height of Japanese expansion in the South Pacific had some 200 radio outlets, including Manila, Singapore, New Guinea, Batavia (now Jakarta, in Java, in what is now Indonesia), and Saigon. This covered parts of four time zones. Further complications grew out of the testimony of radio expert Kiwamu Monotsuka, who stated that a number of broadcasts were made at the same time and on the same frequencies, from Tokyo and from transmitters located in other Far East cities, so it was possible to hear a number of women on the air simultaneously.[57]

Collins encouraged ex-servicemen to state categorically having heard Mrs. D'Aquino at a specific hour, and then would demonstrate that they had been located at a spot from one to three hours off from Tokyo time, and therefore could not possibly have heard the defendant, since it had been established that her stint on Radio Tokyo was always at the same hour.[58]

Not only were prosecution witnesses hopelessly mired, testifying to hearing other women talking at times before or after it was known when Mrs. D'Aquino was on the air. Later defense witnesses, known in reportorial shorthand as "SWLs," short wave listeners, added much informative testimony on the complicated Japanese radio scene in the Pacific. It was one, Gustave C. Gallagher of San Francisco, an indefatigable eavesdropper on Japanese broadcasts the whole war, who estimated Radio Tokyo outlets to be at least 200, while another, one May Hagedorn of Everett, Washington, declared that she had heard at least six different women broadcasting news from Tokyo, as well as other women announcers on Japanese radio from Manila, Java and Saigon.[59] Jordan has concluded that "There may have been as many as two dozen 'Tokyo Roses' broadcasting during the war," including several who had been born in the US. Like many other people, he has been puzzled as to why only one of them was ever tried.[60]

A side issue of this line of investigation sank in importance as the complex picture of Japanese radio was exposed to view. There had been much said in earlier months of 340 broadcasts which had been done at Radio Tokyo and transcribed on discs (but only one of which was a complete Zero Hour broadcast), and which were in the hands of the Government at one time in the investigation of Mrs. D'Aquino. By this stage of the trial only 13 were left. Where were the others, which had figured so prominently in the early bombast? Somehow or other they had been subjected to routine destruction, the authorities explained. Tamba maintained, however, that these recordings had never been destroyed, but actually were stored right there in San Francisco, at the army base in the Presidio. He entertained the suspicion that the recordings were suppressed evidence by the Government which would prove the defendant innocent as charged.

The jurors were excused July 29 while the judge, attorneys, reporters and the defendant spent the day listening to these remaining discs, (by now the total had been reduced to 6), those done reputedly by 'Orphan Ann,' whose voice Mrs. D'Aquino already admitted was hers. These were officially prosecution Exhibits 16-21. Two other witnesses asserted that the voices were the same,[61] which did not prove anything, since it was now a substantive matter: what had she *said*?

Mrs. D'Aquino became ill and the trial was recessed from August 4 to August 8. Thereafter another Japanese witness, Satoshi Nakamura, master of ceremonies on Zero Hour, took the stand, and while testifying that the defendant had not been coerced to broadcast under the name 'Orphan Ann,' challenged the veracity of a succession of previous prosecution witnesses, denying she had ever uttered any of the 14 inflammatory remarks on the program which they had attributed to her. This performance characterized the sustained series of contradictory confrontations heard all during the trial. Nakamura further testified that Mrs. D'Aquino had been employed entirely in simple disc jockey work, introducing recordings and the like, and had not read news or political commentary.[62]

De Wolfe summed up the Government's contentions thereafter and on August 12 rested his case.[63] Judge Roche denied a defense motion for acquittal argued by associate defense counsel Olshausen on August 11,[64] and the trial resumed with the defense introducing its witnesses.

The seventh week of the trial was the dramatic and emotional high point. Preceded by a 40-minute opening statement to the jury by Tamba, the defense put on the stand both Cousens and then Major Ince. Cousens, a radio announcer in Sydney, Australia by that time, came to the defense of Mrs. D'Aquino in an earnest manner, and both he and Ince denied *in toto* the series of 'morale-damaging' statements attributed to her by previous prosecution witnesses. Ince, corroborating Cousens' stand, reiterated his distrust of all Japanese connected with the Zero Hour show, whether native or US-born, his suspicion of the defendant resulting in his not allowing any information of any significance to get in their hands.[65] Cousens was on the stand a long time, but despite De Wolfe's persistence stuck to his blanket denial that she had said any of the things the prosecution alleged.[66]

The Government had a little better luck with Reyes, the remaining member of the Zero Hour trio, who testified for four days in the eighth week of the trial. Reyes was now a student at Vanderbilt University. De Wolfe, who treated Reyes in a shabby and contemptuous way, succeeded in pointing out that he contradicted in part what Cousins and Ince said previously, in statements he had given the FBI in October, 1948. But Reyes insisted that he had been intimidated into signing these statements by agents Tillman and Dunn after 20 hours of questioning in four separate sessions.[67] Reyes further observed that while being questioned he could see the dimensions of the case being built against Mrs. D'Aquino, and thought that, if established, he could be subjected to a similar trial if returned to the Philippines. He further asserted while on the stand that FBI interrogators had threatened to turn him over to Philippine counter-intelligence.[68]

After a succession of other defense witnesses, including one J.F. Whitten, who testified that he had heard 'Tokyo Rose' in 1942,[69] long before the employment of Mrs. D'Aquino, and the defendant's husband, Felipe

D'Aquino, who declared that she had made public statements in Japan predicting Japanese defeat, or had lauded an American victory,[70] Mrs. D'Aquino took the stand herself September 7, 8 and 9. On these three days she repeated many of the facts appearing at the start of this account, again denying ever making political commentary. She called attention once more to the other female announcers on Radio Tokyo, while re-stating her record of friendly and helpful association with various prisoners of war.[71]

Just prior to her testimony, depositions by persons in Japan were introduced, one from the defendant's landlady, Mrs. Funane Kido, which quoted Mrs. D'Aquino saying "Japan hasn't a chance in the world of winning the war" (The defendant lived with Mrs. Kido from October, 1944 to September, 1945).[72]

Probably the most important deposition relating to the case of the defense that the defendant was being charged with being a large number of women radio personalities was that of Ken Murayama. New York born in 1911 and a graduate of George Washington University, Murayama had gone to Japan in 1939 and become a Japanese national. In 1949 a translator of moving pictures in Tokyo, he had written scripts for radio during the war, mainly for a so-called 'torch-singer' named Myrtle Liston, a Philippines national, who broadcast from Manila and was known among American troops as 'Manila Rose.' Murayama admitted that he wrote material for her which specifically "sought to create homesickness among allied troops" in the Pacific.[73] But this barely introduced a far larger situation, the Pacific-wide spread of Japanese wartime radio and its multiplicity of English-speaking women announcers and newscasters.

Though it was fairly well established by now that the defendant had not been employed in enterprises such as those of 'Manila Rose' and others elsewhere, nevertheless, the prosecutor, De Wolfe, was described in an Associated Press story on September 14 as having subjected Mrs. D'Aquino to a 'hammering crossfire,' which went on for three days, seeking by this pounding to get her to admit that she had been employed to make American servicemen in the Pacific homesick. But he failed to get her to admit anything of this sort.[74]

The defense made its final argument September 21[75]; the Government's summation was completed September 23.[76] The jury was charged, and began its deliberations, and after four days, on the evening of September 29, the Associated Press reported that "a somewhat reluctant federal court jury" had found Iva Toguri D'Aquino guilty of treason on a single one of the eight counts. The jury foreman, John W. Mann, of Oakland, an employe of a glass-making concern, was quoted as saying that the jury would have liked to acquit the defendant, but "we did the only thing we thought possible under the judge's instructions."[77] To the critics of the trial, these instructions were simply the crowning irregularity in a trial which blossomed with irregularities.

A private poll of the reporters covering the trial had resulted in a 9-1 vote for acquittal. When told this, Mann replied that the jury was of about the same sentiment. At one time it had only one person for conviction; at another, the vote stood 10-2 for acquittal.[78] The jury had been harangued for nearly two hours by the judge prior to the commencement of its deliberations,[79] and kept coming back for copies of the transcript of the testimony of Oki, Mitsushio and Clark Lee.[80]

After the third return of the jury, Judge Roche lectured them on the necessity of coming to a verdict,[81] stressing the cost of the trial, and the economic consequences to the Government of an inconclusive result, with vague overtones to the effect that it was their 'patriotic duty' to arrive at a verdict, as some editorial commentators put it, subsequently. So, as a consequence of this set of instructions from the bench, what should have been at worst a hung jury was turned into a conviction.[82] When Jordan observed that Judge Roche had been "little credit to the federal bench," there were students of the proceedings who thought that he had uttered the understatement of the last quarter of a century.

And it was on the grounds of this amended set of instructions to the jury being prejudicial that Atty. Collins announced that the conviction would be appealed, to the Ninth District Court. A testy and spirited fighter, Collins stated flatly that the trial had "resulted in more instances of reversible error than any other trial in American judicial history."[83]

Before pronouncing sentence, Judge Roche in rapid order denied four defense motions introduced to set aside the conviction. These consisted of a request for a new trial, on the grounds that the instructions to the jury were technically illegal and that the prosecutor had been guilty of misconduct during the trial; a request for "arrest of judgment," on the grounds that the indictment did not state a public offense, and also on the grounds that the Federal Court in San Francisco had no jurisdiction in the case, and that the defendant should have been tried in Okinawa, since that location of American jurisdiction was the first which the defendant had touched on leaving Japan; a call for acquittal, on grounds of insufficient evidence and that the defendant was either in double jeopardy or that her year in jail in Japan before her return to the U.S. constituted a violation of her constitutional right to a speedy trial; a plea for clemency, and the five-year minimum sentence accompanying this.

Then he sentenced Mrs. D'Aquino to ten years in prison, a fine of $10,000 and loss of her U.S. citizenship.[84]

So ended the longest and most expensive treason trial in US history to that time, lasting over 12 weeks, totalling 56 courtroom days, and 40 hours of deliberation by the jury, covering a period of four days. During the trial the prosecution had called up to 46 witnesses, the defense 25, and depositions had been filed from 19 witnesses who remained in Japan.

The Alameda (Calif.) *Times Star* on October 1 editorially called for a new trial, on the grounds that the exclusion of non-whites from the jury, and the judge's pressure on the jury to come to a verdict by stressing the likely cost of another trial, were prejudicial. The logic of Judge Roche's position, it appeared to them, was that there was a price tag on justice.

Colonel Hada, who resumed his education after retiring from the army, submitted a master's degree thesis to the history faculty at the University of San Francisco in May, 1973 titled "The Indictment and Trial of Iva Ikuko Toguri D'Aquino—'Tokyo Rose,' " 200 pages in length with appendices totalling another 200, in which he concluded that the case had been "studded with bribery, perjury, kidnapping, unlawful imprisonment, destruction of records, . . ." as well as the defendant being "a casualty of our judicial system which failed to protect her fundamental rights."

It was fitting that the 'Tokyo Rose' trial should terminate a short while after Owen Cunningham, a Des Moines lawyer who had served as defense counsel to the Japanese ambassador to Germany, General Hiroshi Oshima, in one of the lamentable "war crimes" trials, told a Lincoln, Nebraska Bar Association audience that Oshima's trial had been a "comedy of errors."[85]

The striking thing about the vast efforts and expenditures of the prosecution was the miserable tidbit of material it used to send Mrs. D'Aquino to jail for ten years while fining her $10,000. Its vainglorious brandishing of 340 recordings, deflated to 18, then 13, to 8, and finally 6, then was pinched down to *a mere 25 words allegedly uttered on a single one*! This ridiculous progression downward did indicate the malicious zeal of the prosecution, however, and the frantic clutching at anything to justify its sensational charges.

The words which were ultimately decided to be 'treasonous' consisted of the following, spoken after the naval battle of Leyte Gulf in October, 1944 when the radio voice remarked,[86]

> 'Now you fellows have lost all your ships. You are really orphans of the Pacific. How do you think you are going to get home?'

And it was on the say-so of Japanese nationals Oki and Mitsushio that they were credited to Mrs. D'Aquino. No one thought it strange that not a single U.S. citizen had presented evidence of treason by her that the court would accept. (There is an interesting related matter which did not seem to come to anyone's attention: *if* Mrs. D'Aquino *had read* the fateful words, who had *written* them, and why was this not as important, in a legal process trying to establish treasonous behavior?)

In view of the outpourings of pro-Communist billingsgate issued by Americans from Hanoi during the Vietnam war which hardly drew a rebuke, what was used to send Iva Toguri D'Aquino to jail under heavy fine was a laughable travesty. (And for the Government to maintain, and for any member of the jury to believe, that any American would take credence in a news broadcast to the effect that their entire fleet had been sunk, was a towering insult to the intelligence of even the least-gifted member of the entire American armed forces.) But in this manner was the Government's brontosaurus reduced to the size of a gnat.

Prosecutor De Wolfe's smug dictum that the jury's verdict was "a just one for the United States"[87] contained an overtone of panic. Obviously, there were people in high political rank who wanted this woman convicted, even on the flimsiest evidence, which turned out to be the case. That a jury should consider the 25 words on which their decision hinged "sufficiently damaging to American morale to constitute treason" was a rationalization of the weakest and most pathetic kind.

Why the Government was so anxious to convict Mrs. D'Aquino is still puzzling, however. It might be laid to the motive of indulging in additional vengeance against a defeated enemy, which surely was behind most of the preposterous 'war crimes' trials. But Mrs. D'Aquino was a native born American, which the prosecution spent much time seeing to that such was firmly planted in the record. The reasons for the persistent harrassment and repeated jailings of this woman, until a long and very expensive trial could be engineered to lodge her in a cell even longer, may take much time to unravel. It would appear, however, that some involuted point of high statecraft, and not personal malice toward the defendant, was at the base of their motivation.

Atty. Collins denounced Mrs. D'Aquino's conviction as "absolutely erroneous – unsupportable by any credible testimony."[88] His efforts to undo this lamentable proceedings began immediately, and, to the surprise of many, his labors to gain for his client a full presidential pardon continued until his death on July 16, 1974.[89] A reporter, interviewing him and his colleague Tamba (who preceded him in death, in the second week of December, 1973), and Mrs. D'Aquino, in San Francisco in the summer of 1973, related that her lawyers[90]

> continue to stand by her after 23 years, and insist that she is innocent of treason. Moreover, they charge that she was and is the victim of public hysteria, racial discrimination, and political vengeance by postwar American officials. 'Without any question,' said Collins angrily, 'she should be pardoned, and compensated by Congress.'

It was expected that the court would deny defense motions for a new trial. Following the sentencing, an appeal was filed and Mrs. D'Aquino's release on bail was sought. Federal District Court denied bail shortly after the appeal was filed.[91] (Only convicted Stalinist spies such as Judith Coplon seemed to deserve release on bail.)[92] Mrs. D'Aquino's sentence began November 3, 1949, and she was transferred from San Francisco on November 15 to start her prison term in the facility at Alderson, West Virginia.[93]

"Judicial processes do not take place in a social void," cautioned Professor Arthur M. Schlesinger, Sr., in his introduction to George Louis Joughin's and Edmund M. Morgan's *The Legacy of Sacco and Vanzetti*.[94] But at the time he wrote that, he and the legions of his fellow liberals were part of a dominant climate of opinion which reflected little more than smug self-satisfaction at what was happening to Iva Toguri D'Aquino, for to protest on their part would have cast a shadow on a portion of the propaganda of what had been acclaimed boastfully by Stanley High as "The Liberals' War."[95]

Supreme Court Justice William O. Douglas, in February, 1950, conceded the issue of whether Mrs. D'Aquino had had a fair trial and been the beneficiary of proper legal guarantees was a debatable one,[96] but in general the legal Establishment supported the outcome of the 1949 trial. Mrs. D'Aquino appealed her conviction in September of that year, and the appeal was argued in March, 1951. A U.S. Circuit Court upheld her conviction on October 10, 1951. When she asked the Appeals Court to reconsider her appeal rejection, a rehearing was denied December 17. When the case was taken to the Supreme Court, the appeal was rejected April 28, 1952 and on April 6, 1953 the Supreme Court barred any further review of the case.[97]

But the matter was not ended, nor were the travails of Mrs. D'Aquino over. On January 28, 1956 she was freed from federal prison after serving six years and two months of her original sentence.[98] Justice Department officials literally met her on the steps of the prison and forced her to sign an alien registration card, informing her that she would be deported as an undesirable alien. Only then did the American Civil Liberties Union begin to get into the act. (There was a basic contradiction here: an alien cannot be tried for treason, and a native born American cannot be deported. The Government wanted to scramble these: for the purposes of the treason trial, the prosecution had been tireless in its concentration on her U.S. citizenship, but after her conviction wished to view her as a deportable alien.)

Now the Immigration and Naturalization Service appeared on the scene, announcing their decision to try to have her deported, though they admitted having no precedent upon which to call in seeking to bring about the denaturalization and deportation of a native-born citizen. There was a law passed in 1940 which stipulated that a U.S. national, whether by birth or naturalization, would be deprived of American nationality upon conviction for treason, but the geniuses who put this together did not make clear how a native born person could be deported anywhere. Mrs. D'Aquino had not come from Japan. If she was to be sent there, then the Immigration Service were apparently going to invoke an ethnic clause of their own invention, which apparently implied immense consequences for the future.[99] Nor could the technicality of possessing foreign citizenship be rung in, since she possessed neither Japanese nor Portuguese citizenship.

The press was miffed that she showed "no repentance" upon release from prison,[100] and reporters were not charmed by her pluck in her announced decision to fight deportation.[101] Now living in Chicago, the Government authorities ordered her movement restricted to a 50-mile radius of that city.[102] By now there were people in the country who thought the Government was rubbing things in, and demonstrating malice beyond normal expectations. An American Legion post in Springfield, Ohio, a most unlikely source of support, even urged the President, now Mr. Eisenhower, to pardon her.[103] A month later the immigration authorities ordered her to leave the USA voluntarily within a month or face deportation, again not too sure where she could be sent.[104]

Then the ice floe began to melt a bit. The following month, April 12, 1956, she was permitted to move to San Francisco again,[105] where her deportation hearing was supposed to begin April 26,[106] But the hearing never took place. The matter dragged on and on for over two years. the Government finally dropping the deportation efforts on July 10, 1958.[107]

But the threat of it being reopened remained. And if Mrs. D'Aquino were to leave the country voluntarily, there existed the possibility that she would not be allowed to return. The federal bureaucracy still housed people who were embarrassed by the continuation of this case. And the venom was little abated in some circles 25 years after the trial. In the interview in the summer of 1973, published in the *Christian Science Monitor*, Mrs. D'Aquino remarked, "Everytime the case is recalled in the papers, I seem to hear from every maniac in the country—everything from marriage proposals to death threats."

Meanwhile, the 'Tokyo Rose' affair took other directions, now that the phase involving the prison sentence had been liquidated. Mrs. D'Aquino's indefatigable legal defenders, Collins and Tamba, pursued the avenue of petitions of executive clemency for their client. Tamba filed the first on June 7, 1954 during Dwight D. Eisenhower's first term in office, while she was still in prison. The second was presented to President Lyndon B. Johnson by Collins on November 4, 1968, the day before Richard M. Nixon won the election of that year. Neither petition received an answer.[108]

In the case of the Government, pursuit of the defendant took shape in an equally tireless effort to collect the $10,000 fine which had been assessed by Judge Roche in October, 1949. There was no pronounced attempt of this sort until 1968, when it may have been further aggravated by the executive clemency petition, in re-opening the entire affair. About half the amount was paid prior to 1971, at which time the Justice Department once more applied pressure to collect the remainder. Haled into Federal Court in Chicago, Mrs. D'Aquino was subjected to a demand for the $5,255 unpaid balance. Collins, associate defense counsel in this action, heatedly up-braided the Government for its 'capricious harassment' of his client, and wished an explanation for the heavy-handed harrying of this long-badgered woman for such a small sum of money. He noted the far different attitude toward many others who owed unpaid fines in the billions of dollars and which the Government never tried to collect.[109]

As late as the closing weeks of 1972, collection agents of the Nixon administration were assiduously at work trying to attach her wages for this unpaid balance. Mrs. D'Aquino's request for a hearing as a preliminary to getting the federal authorities to stop this planned looting of her income at the source was denied by an imperious panel of federal judges in Chicago on November 15, 1972.[110]

In 1975 Jun Toguri, Mrs. D'Aquino's father, died. His will contained a provision stipulating that the remainder of his daughter's fine was to be paid out of the estate. The amount was collected to the last cent and the Government finally closed the case.[111]

So ended the sustained prosecution of Iva Ikuko Toguri D'Aquino after a period of 30 years, spanning the administrations of six different presidents. The story is not yet concluded, however. The faint and tremulous efforts on Mrs. D'Aquino's behalf dating from the late 1950s took somewhat more solid shape finally on July 27, 1974, when the Japanese American Citizens League first took positive and official action in announcing their support for her and formally resolved that it would "use its leadership, manpower, and resources to correct the miscarriage of justice in Iva Toguri's case by seeking all executive or other remedies available under the law."[112] And there is another aspect of continuity in the situation, as Atty. Wayne

Collins, Jr., son of Mrs. D'Aquino's original chief defense counsel, headed the campaign to obtain for her a presidential pardon, which began with a nationwide publicity drive by the JACL early in 1976. He announced that he would file this third application for executive clemency after the election in November, 1976.[113]

On November 17 the petition for a presidential pardon was filed by Mrs. D'Aquino in San Francisco. An atmosphere of symbolism prevailed, in that the petition, addressed to the U.S. Pardon Attorney, was accepted from her personally by San Francisco Postmaster Lim P. Lee on the steps of the former federal court house where she was convicted in 1949. President Gerald R. Ford thus became the third chief executive to whom this procedure for the partial redress of past wrongs was directed. Newspapers across the land treated the event as front page news and followed it with a flurry of special commentaries with incidental references to its history. But for some observers there was the eerie feeling that the past and the present had, at least for a moment, become indivisible.

The "Tokyo Rose" case, like all treason cases, is as much political as it is legal. It is one more illustration that the word 'treason' is far more a political term than it is anything else, and is always subjectively defined and applied by whatever power element happens to be in control of the machinery of the State.[114] In all cases they seek to interpret 'treason' in harmony with their own interests while trying to conceal it all behind the majestic spook of 'national interest.' Looking back at the 'Tokyo Rose' proceedings from the vantage point of a generation, it is obvious why the entire affair had become, in the minds of an increasing number, a circumstance in which, 1) the trial was a lamentable succession of events which cumulatively amounted to a glaring miscarriage of justice, and, 2) the whole proceedings of the Government beginning even before the grand jury indictment, was primarily a glittering press-agent's spectacle, aimed at trying the personification of a World War Two soldier's legend,[115] not a person with civil and constitutional rights, and was therefore little more than a grandiose technical frame-up.*

Mrs. Iva Ikuko Toguri D'Aquino was granted an unconditional pardon by President Gerald R. Ford on the afternoon of his last full official day as the thirty-eighth President of the United States, January 19, 1977.

---

* [The above essay, the third draft of a work begun in 1974, delivered as an oral presentation in 1975 and issued in its first printed form in 1976, was published in March, 1977. Since that time the first full-scale book on the subject has been published by Masayo Duus, *Tokyo Rose: Orphan of the Pacific* (Tokyo, San Francisco and New York: Kodansha International Ltd., 1979). It adds extensive valuable detail as well as much absorbing human interest to the story, and a thorough examination of the trial, though it could have been made somewhat more useful to students of this entire business by the addition of a bibliography of all the known newspaper and magazine stories, and other partial treatments of the 'Tokyo Rose' narrative, in previous books.]

[1]The first draft of this essay was written at the close of 1974 and was read at the same symposium held on the campus of the University of Southern California which heard the first two essays in this collection late in the afternoon of March 9, 1975. A revised draft was submitted to the editors of *Reason* Magazine in July, and accepted for publication by its editors on August 18. It was published in the issue for February, 1976, which became available shortly after New Year's Day.

The decision of the Japanese American Citizens League in 1975 to form the National Committee for Iva Toguri and to start a country-wide drive which they aimed at obtaining for her a presidential pardon led to the parallel production of a booklet titled *Iva Toguri d'Aquino: Victim of a Legend,* published by the JACL in San Francisco with the date September, 1975, though copies did not become generally circulated until about the same time that the essay below was made available across the country by *Reason.*

The first national comment on the re-opening of the 'Tokyo Rose' case by the JACL's Toguri Committee began shortly thereafter, in the first week of February. In the subsequent nine months there was a continuous flow of news stories and editorials prompted by the JACL's campaign news releases and circulation of their booklet. An effort has been made to incorporate in the notes to this essay most of the pertinent published material which has a bearing on the narrative, though it should be pointed out that the only mention of this essay so far noticed in the copious press attention to the pardon proceedings was in the column written by the syndicated columnist Nicholas von Hoffman, published in the New York *Post* on March 10, 1976. There are significant differences between this treatment of the 'Tokyo Rose' case and that found in *Iva Toguri d'Aquino: Victim of a Legend,* since they were prepared under quite different circumstances and not intended for the same purpose, However, in places where they rely on the same source as in the case of the coverage of some parts of the actual trial, there is obviously a similar flavor at least in part. Though written under totally independent auspices, and by writers utterly unaware of one another, the coincidence is that both were nationally distributed at about the same week.

This version contains considerable updating based on newly revealed information and also includes the full original documentation, which also has been amplified by additional data recently made known by subsequent investigators, none of which was present in the previously published version for obvious space reasons. New material added to the documentation is enclosed in brackets.

[2][The New York *Times* on August 29, 1975 published a lengthy front page story on the trials of 'war criminals' in Germany thirty years after the end of World War Two, calling attention to thousands of cases still pending and to the hundreds of prosecutors and judges still assigned to them.]

[3]It is earnestly hoped that those ignorant of the matter do not have to depend on works such as John Toland's *The Rising Sun* (New York: Random House, 1970). The errors and omission of pertinent facts make it a prime source of misinformation, though it is far outmatched by the account of Brig. Gen. Elliott R. Thorpe, *East Wind, Rain* (Boston: Gambit, 1969), pp. 224-227, a hash of fact and fiction which manages to obscure or misconceive every important point in the basic story. Students of the matter had expectations of a far superior account from the man who was chief of counter-intelligence on the staff of Gen. Douglas MacArthur and whose office handled the case of Iva Toguri from the start. (Gen. Thorpe spells her name "Tuguri" throughout.)

[4]The inflaming of both the Japanese and Americans by atrocity stories at various stages of the Pacific War had a bearing eventually on the 'Tokyo Rose' proceedings. During the invasion of the Philippines by Japanese forces in December, 1941, after the attack on Hawaii, there were repeated charges made by Japanese radio and telegraphic agencies of indiscriminate and mass killing of Japanese civilians in the Philippines by American troops. These became so frequent that some American newspaper editors became annoyed and made public announcements to their readers that they would not print any more of them.

Early in January, 1942 after the capture of Manila the American papers front-paged charges that U.S. civilians were being 'treated harshly' by the Japanese, though General Douglas MacArthur's war communique #44 mentioned only that Americans in the city were ordered to remain indoors during certain hours of the day. And American papers printed in very lavish display, beginning in 1944, official U.S. charges of atrocities committed on American troops who surrendered to Japan in April, 1942, in Bataan, a district across the bay from Manila. The "Bataan death march" was, next to the prodigious extravaganza devoted to the captured German concentration camps some months later, the most thoroughly exploited atrocity incident by USA agencies of public information. Thus, Japanese misdeeds in the war in the Pacific were given the maximum promotion, and contributed extensively in incubating a fierce racial hostility among the general run of Americans. The parallel policy of blacking out entirely the counter-charges of Japan of massacre of their civilian nationals and even their prisoners of war helped to fix the belief in the onesided nature of wartime excesses, which is the delight of any national propaganda operators if they can achieve it. What was not calculated was the long hangover of this kind of public conditioning, and it was obvious during the 1949 trial of Iva Toguri D'Aquino that a potent Japanophobia still bubbled through the structure of American society. See Note 18.

[5]A disdainful estimate of the Japanese enemy was reported to the American populace as late as the end of 1941 from the Philippines, where the war spread after Pearl Harbor. Associated Press stories filed from Manila by Clark Lee on December 26 and December 29, and front-paged in a number of American newspapers, disparaged the invading Japanese troops as 15 to 18 year old boys, dressed half in civilian clothes, poorly armed, and ineffective. Lee repeated the belittling estimates of American officers who considered their soldiers to be equal to five or six of the invaders. Toland, in his *The Rising Sun* (p. 246), blamed the American officers exclusively for these grave underestimations of Japanese soldiers, alleging that Lee was just repeating in print what they told him. Toland entirely overlooked Lee's low opinion of the Japanese as expressed in his first book (see below). In view of Lee's years of watching the Japanese soldiers in China, where they rarely if ever lost a battle with the Chinese, especially Mao Tse-tung's Reds, he certainly knew better than to give credence to the preposterous low-grading of Japanese soldiery which found its way into his dispatches to the U.S.A. from the Philippines in December, 1941.

[The saga of Clark Gould Lee almost rivals that of his famous prey, Iva Toguri. Born in Oakland, California (the Associated Press managed to assign at least three different birth years to him in various editorial profiles during the early years of World War Two), he was a graduate of Rutgers University and went to work for the AP in 1929. Married to a Hawaiian princess directly descended, reputedly, from Queen Lilioukalani, Lee had served in several distant outposts of the AP news service, and had come from Shanghai to the Philippines just before the American phase of the Pacific War began. *Newsweek* (January 19, 1942, pp. 61-62) described him as "an amiable six-footer" who had escaped Manila a short time ahead of advancing columns of Japanese troops and managed to get to the American fortification on Corregidor "after a two-day trip over mountain trails and heavily bombed roads." From here and other points in the Philippines, Lee filed a long succession of stories to America, mainly by radio, which were frequently displayed on the front pages of newspapers all over the land.

The Second World War brought about a magic transformation of some reporters into 'war correspondents,' and Lee became one of the most glamorous of all. He was the principal inventor of the style of war reporting which primarily emphasized the exploits of the common soldier, accompanied by the pinpointing of his name and home in the U.S.A. It was an extremely popular approach with Army public relations, and was eventually brought to a high polish by another Pacific correspondent, Ernie Pyle.

Lee eventually escaped to Australia shortly before the Japanese captured the Philippines in 1942, and subsequently reported the Pacific campaigns to the final victory over Japan in the late summer of 1945. The Associated Press considered even Lee's movement from one location to another in 1942 to be news. A general story almost a column long about his arrival in Melbourne in late March appeared in many American newspapers. The AP also boasted that the Army spokesmen had praised his reports on the war as the best written "on any front." He incorporated his reportage of the first year of American combat in the South Pacific in a book, *They Call It Pacific: An Eyewitness Story of Our War Against Japan from Bataan to the Solomons,* which was published by Viking in New York in March, 1943. Lee came back to the U.S. late in 1942 and apparently completed this book while home. In it he revealed immense contempt for the Japanese, whom he considered "primitive people." In his three years in Shanghai he was a reporter at times accompanying the Japanese army in periodic operations in China, on which occasions he teamed with Harry Brundidge, then employed by the St. Louis *Star-Times (They Call It Pacific,* pp. 279-280); presumably their close association began at this time. His second book, *One Last Look Around* (New York: Duell, Sloan and Pearce, 1947) was largely devoted to gloating over the wrecked and blackened Japan he triumphantly entered almost as soon as the first wave of occupying American troops, in search of his principal objectives, the first interviews with Premier Tojo and the girl known as 'Tokyo Rose.' (See note 6.) He again had the opportunity to run much of what he had to say about the latter past the trial of 1949, at which he was a star Government witness. Three years later he co-authored with Richard Henschel the book *Douglas MacArthur* (New York: Holt, 1952).

Clark Lee died of a heart attack at his home in Pebble Beach, California, where he had lived since 1946, on February 15, 1953. The Associated Press said he was 46 years old (See New York *Times* obituary, February 16, 1953, p. 21; the Associated Press obituary was published in the Colorado Springs *Gazette Telegraph*, February 16, 1953, p. 10.)]

[6]Theodore Tamba, active as counsel for the defense for almost 25 years, and a keen student of the social context of the trial, was convinced that Winchell and Kate Smith, who took the lead after the war in demanding Iva Toguri's prosecution despite two government departments having cleared her of treason charges, actually believed there was only one 'Tokyo Rose' and that she was the defendant. Furthermore, since there was talk for a spell of launching 'Tokyo Rose' on American radio, in view of her formidable popularity with returned Pacific servicemen. Tamba concluded that both her radio personality accusers feared that should she essay upon a radio career in the US, she might eclipse them in popularity.

[But many Americans were crestfallen to learn that there was no lone "sexpot broadcaster," and even Clark Lee, the first sensationalizer of the main character in the 'Tokyo Rose' story, Iva Toguri, conceded in his 1947 book, *One Last Look Around* (New York: Duell, Sloan and Pearce), that she was "a pleasant-looking girl, but by no stretch of the imagination a siren." As for the reputation for having a sultry, suggestive voice, her husband, Felipe D'Aquino, thought it closely compared instead to the flat and angular intonation of "Molly," of the "Fibber McGee and Molly" radio show, one of the most popular of its kind in the USA. (Concerning Lee's book, his second on the Pacific war, one should consult the blistering review by Capt. P.J. Searles in the New York *Herald Tribune Weekly Book Review* for June 8, 1947). As for the social history of the United States between December 1941 and August, 1945, such efforts as have been made fall far from a fairly accurate picture of the total situation, and even the daily press reflects only a fragmentary documentation of innovations in American social life which in part were on an order about which no one in Japan could have more than imagined.]

[7]The basic facts concerning Iva Toguri D'Aquino and her family are to be found in the FBI statement taken by agent Frederick G. Tillman from her on April 30, 1946, which was read into the record at the trial, and the testimony of Mrs. D'Aquino herself while on the stand September 7-9, 1949. [An excellent summary can be found in Japanese American Citizens League, *Iva Toguri d'Aquino: Victim of a Legend* (San Francisco, 1975; second edition, 1976), hereinafter cited as JACL, *Iva Toguri*. The texts of the two editions are virtually identical, but the second edition contains valuable bibliographical references not listed in the first.]

[8]Related by the defendant at the trial; see *Pacific Citizen*, September 10, 1949; (see note 42.) See also account by David Holmstrom, published in *Christian Science Monitor* for August 18, 1973, subsequently reprinted in San Bernardino (Calif.) *Sun Telegram* for November 1, 1973.

[9]Essential to an understanding of this episode are the books by Michi Weglyn, *Years of Infamy: The Untold Story of America's Concentration Camps* (New York: Morrow, 1976) and Allan R. Bosworth, *America's Concentration Camps* (New York: Norton, 1967), latter also published in a paper cover edition by Bantam Books the following year. These should be supplemented with *Exile of a Race* by Anne Reeploeg Fisher (Seattle: F & T Publishers, 1965) (the author maintains that before 1941 more Japanese had come to America from and around Hiroshima than from any other place in Japan), and Eugene V. Rostow, "Our Worst Wartime Mistake," *Harper's Magazine*, September, 1945, pp. 193-201. Rostow, then a law professor at Yale, said of them, "One hundred thousand persons were sent to concentration camps on a record which wouldn't support a conviction for stealing a dog," though his liberal blinders prevent him from accurately pinpointing the persons whose decisions were basically responsible for this program. Mrs. Weglyn's research amply takes care of such omissions in Rostow's account.

[10]For an elaboration on this and related matters below, see the lengthy Associated Press account of the defendant's testimony, in Colorado Springs *Gazette Telegraph*, September 9, 1949, p. 3 [and also the section "Abandonment and Survival (1942-1943)," in JACL, *Iva Toguri*, p. 5].

[11]Cousens, captured at Singapore in 1942, and Ince and Reyes, captured when Corregidor in the Philippines surrendered in the same year, along with a fourth participant, Kenneth Parkyns, an Australian flier shot down over New Guinea, were all experienced radio broadcasters. [Reyes was actually well known in Hawaii and the Philippines, since it was he who had read over the radio the announcements of the capitulation of Bataan and Corregidor in April, 1942 from a tunnel of a bunker on the latter, a message which was repeated on radio in the United States later. Reyes was sent to Japan at the direct request of Japanese army propaganda directors, after having been imprisoned with Ince in Fort Santiago in Manila following capture. See note 67.]

[12][The Zero Hour sound engineer, Teruo Ozasa, pointed out that there were several other programs being beamed out of Radio Tokyo from the same building at the same time. One of these was called the Hinomaru (Rising Sun) Hour, which also utilized prisoners of war and which did broadcast "statements designed to demoralize American troops," he recalled. He also directed attention to another English language program, produced by the German Embassy in the studios of Radio Tokyo, called the German Hour, which "Employed several English-speaking women to taunt GIs." For additional materials on and comments by Ozasa, see note 58.]

[13]The title of this thesis was "The Effects of the Broadcasts of 'Tokyo Rose' During World War II." Since we know that American servicemen called all women broadcasters on Japanese radio 'Tokyo Rose,' regardless of which one it was or from which Asian city she spoke, and since it is recognized that some of them read propaganda or other material with a morale-damaging intent, the impact upon Americans other than providing entertainment must be judged to be nearly imperceptible.

[14]The earliest assertion of an American serviceman listening to 'Tokyo Rose' which has come to the attention of this writer is that of Navy Commander Wilmer Thompson at Pearl Harbor, the week after the Japanese attack in December, 1941. Editors of the *Army Times*, *Pearl Harbor and Hawaii: A Military History* (New York: Bonanza Books, 1971), p. 123.

[15][Iva Toguri's career on the Zero Hour began with a broadcast on the evening of November 13, 1943, according to JACL, *Iva Toguri*, p. 6. The script was written by her prisoner of war associates.]

[16]Documentation on 'Tokyo Rose' is very sketchy during the peak of the war years, compared to the immense volume of gossip and story-telling which is primarily an oral tradition. The New York *Times* published stories in March and May, 1944 which mentioned 'Tokyo Rose' being a 'favorite' of Pacific servicemen, though they were utterly unimpressed by the general content of Japanese radio propaganda. The fateful Leyte Gulf 'Tokyo Rose' broadcast was also reported in the *Times* on October 30. The obviously fallacious nature of this 'newscast' drew more attention in the U.S.A. than anything else ever reported on Radio Tokyo, and undoubtedly this publicity had a part to play in it being ballooned into a matter of great consequence in the trial of 1949. But the conclusion of the *Times* in deflating Japanese radio propaganda to insignificance in 1944 contradicted the view of the 'Tokyo Rose' jury that the Leyte Gulf broadcast undermined American morale. One may assume however that this latter conclusion may have been more an ex post facto gloss thrown in to rationalize in part their sudden 180-degree turn on the status of the defendant; see 'New York *Times*, March 27, 1944, p. 4; May 24, 1944, p. 5; October 30, 1944, p. 3.

[17]Associated Press story, Colorado Springs *Evening Telegraph*, September 10, 1945, p. 1.

[18]Associated Press story, Colorado Springs *Evening Telegraph*, September 18, 1945, main story, page 1, under 72-point banner-headline. The copious promotion of atrocity stories against the Japanese, beginning in China in 1937, accelerating sharply in the Philippines in 1941, and becoming a Noah-type flood from points all over East Asia in 1944-1945, undoubtedly had the effect in the U.S.A. of narcotizing public opinion to the degree that the overwhelming part of the total population, then, and now, looked, and still look, on the atom bombing of Hiroshima and Nagasaki as incidentals and bagatelles, if not not-severe-enough retaliation. The self-righteousness of Americans toward the Japanese lasted a long while after the end of hostilities, despite the world uproar that tended to rise over the atomization of the above Japanese cities. As late as July 23, 1949 one could read sentiments such as the following expressed by Alvah C. Carpenter, chief of the legal section of American occupation headquarters in Tokyo: "Japan will have to earn its way back into the international community." International News Service story, in Colorado Springs *Gazette Telegraph*, July 24, 1949, p. 6-C.

[19]Dopking, "Where Did 'Tokyo Rose' Go? Americans in Japan Wonder," Colorado Springs *Gazette Telegraph*, September 2, 1945, p. 3; New York *Times*, September 1, 1945. p. 4.

[20]Lee and Brundidge worked for separate properties of the Wm. Randolph Hearst publications empire: the International News Service, Lee's affiliation now, and *Cosmopolitan* both belonged to the stable of the Lord of San Simeon. The editors of the latter refused to print Brundidge's account of their joint interview of Iva Toguri, professing to be appalled at the thought of paying money to a "traitor" (the two had promised to pay her $2000. for exclusive rights to her story.) It would appear that this is the earliest instance of her pre-conviction by the American press. The circulation of the rejection is what is believed to have angered Brundidge and led to his allegation of her treasonous behavior to Army intelligence. Brundidge's flair for the sensational was an established character trait. He testified before the Chicago grand jury investigating the murder of newspaperman Alf L. "Jake" Lingle, on June 9, 1930, declaring that the notorious gangland chief Alphonse "Scarface Al" Capone had said that the Chicago police knew the identity of Lingle's killer. Capone denied having said this. New York *Times*, July 19, 1930, p. 3.

[21] In his report from Yokohama on her arrest by an Eighth Army intelligence officer, Merlin Spencer of the Associated Press made no mention of how she had been apprehended, and cited only that she was being held at General Headquarters "for questioning and investigation." Colorado Springs *Evening Telegraph*, September 5, 1945, p. 3; see also New York *Times*, September 6 and September 9, 1945. In this instance and earlier, the *Times* persisted in spelling the family name "Togori."

An NEA telephoto of the accused in her cap and gown at the 1940 UCLA commencement, described as "one of five young women reported to be 'Tokyo Rose,'" was published in newspapers shortly after her arrest. The one examined was on page 16 of the Colorado Springs *Evening Telegraph* for September 7, 1945.

[22] New York *Times*, September 14, 1945, p. 4; [JACL, *Iva Toguri*, p. 11.]

[23] New York *Times*, October 19, 1945, p. 2.

[24] [The San Francisco *Chronicle* reporters Jerry Carroll and Keith Power in their long 4-column piece "How the Tokyo Rose Myth Was Created," published on February 5, 1976, quoted from "a hitherto undisclosed document discovered by *The Chronicle* in the National Archives in Washington," dated April 17, 1946, in which the American occupation authorities after an investigation decided that Iva Toguri had not committed an offense which was punishable under military law. It cited several facts about her and her predicament in Japan after Pearl Harbor which are part of the account above. It bore the signature of U.S. Attorney James M. Carter, and in the course of announcing the government's decision to drop any plans for prosecuting her, also conceded that 'Tokyo Rose' did not exist, and was essentially " 'a composite with at least a dozen voices.' "

The California film maker, Tony Montanari, who has been at work on a film documentary of the 'Tokyo Rose' affair for the past four years, late in June, 1976 made public a sheaf of documents which he declared had been newly released from Justice Department and Federal Bureau of Investigation files under the Freedom of Information Act. Transcripts of some of them reveal that the Justice Department did not believe the evidence was strong enough to warrant prosecution of Iva Toguri for treason in September, 1946. See comment on this material by Mrs. D'Aquino's current counsel, Wayne Collins, Jr., in the story by Dexter Waugh in the San Francisco *Examiner*, June 24, 1976, p. 8.]

[25] [JACL, *Iva Toguri*, p. 14.]

[26] [JACL, *Iva Toguri*, p. 12.]

[27] New York *Times*, October 19, 1945, p. 2. [There were about 10,000 American born Japanese who spent the war in Japan. For some facts concerning the tangled status of these people see JACL, *Iva Toguri*, pp. 3-5, 7, 9, 12.]

[28] There are conflicting accounts of how Winchell became the self-appointed pursuer of Mrs. D'Aquino. One relates that it was directly as a response to the news release concerning her passport application. Another places the cause for his cultivated pseudo-righteousness upon a belated complaint of a listener of his, a woman whose son had been killed in the Pacific war. She apparently had just become aware that Mrs. D'Aquino was out of prison in Japan. What the death of this woman's son had to do with the status of Mrs. D'Aquino is a mystery, but it did provide another occasion for a dress parade of wartime vindictiveness, no matter how ill-directed. It also provided Winchell, with his obnoxious peephole sensationalist modus operandi, another opportunity to elevate nothing into something. With reference to Kate Smith's part in this hysteria, see note 6.

[29] There is no doubt Winchell had a substantial part to play in turning attention from a protest against Mrs. D'Aquino's return to the U.S.A. to one of re-opening the treason ploy once more, which latter brought Lee and Brundidge back to the scene. It was Winchell who revived interest in their famous 1945 interview with her, now asserting that these two newsmen had obtained a confession, while berating them as bunglers for allegedly losing their notes on this interview. This was not so, since Brundidge still had these notes, and now was motivated to see what new mileage might be wrung from them. On Brundidge's fateful part in the next stage of the 'Tokyo Rose' fabrication more will be said later.

[30] [JACL, *Iva Toguri*, p. 12. Even the Los Angeles City Council passed a resolution opposing her return to the USA, on the grounds that her presence might be subversive to 'loyal' Japanese Americans.]

[31] New York *Times*, December 4, 1947, p. 19.

[32] A remarkably accurate account of the material in the above two paragraphs is that in *Newsweek* for August 30, 1948, p. 20.

[33] [The supporting material by Atty. Hogan and the witnesses is in the Montanari documents; see note 24.]

[34] [A succinct account of the transportation of Mrs. D'Aquino from Japan to the United States and her arraignment, as well as of the legal situation surrounding this operation, can be found in JACL, *Iva Toguri*, p. 13.]

[35] "Sally and Rose," *Time* (August 30, 1948), p. 13. The effort here was to smear Mrs. D'Aquino by the guilt-by-association trick of linking her with Mildred Gillars, known as

"Axis Sally," eventually convicted of making broadcasts from Hitler Germany. Miss Gillars had received a sentence of 10 to 30 years.

[36]"When his superior status is suitably acknowledged by those in power, the man of words usually finds all kinds of lofty reasons for siding with the strong against the weak." Eric Hoffer, *The True Believer* (1951), pp. 132-133.

[After the beating taken by Communism in Spain between 1936 and 1939, and the non-aggression pact between Adolf Hitler and Josef Stalin in August of the latter year, the most traumatic experience of left-wing liberalism in the USA has been the conviction of Alger Hiss for perjury on January 20, 1950, during the second administration of Harry S. Truman. A long succession of anguished appraisals has taken place ever since, the most persuasive of which probably is the Freudian analysis-*cum*-history *Friendship and Fratricide: An Analysis of Whittaker Chambers and Alger Hiss* (New York: Viking, 1967), by Dr. Meyer A. Zeligs. This sophisticated psychoanalytic brief in behalf of Hiss and seriously to the detriment of Hiss's accuser, Chambers, seems to have had the assistance of a veritable Who's Who of American liberalism, from a perusal of the credits, documentation and acknowledgements.

There is no adequate study of the fury of the US press and mass communications media, overwhelmingly liberal, aroused by Richard M. Nixon, the key figure in the investigation of Hiss, which led to his prosecution and conviction. A principal byproduct was the vendetta carried out against Nixon for a quarter of a century, conducted on many fronts and disguised in many ways during his career as congressman, vice president and ultimately president. The culmination of this venomous hostility was the implacable and relentless drive which ballooned the Watergate burglary into the crime of the ages and produced Nixon's resignation, a story without parallel in American public affairs.

The marriage between psychoanalysis and history which became an enterprise in full (if not over-full) bloom in the 1960s continues, and its product still proliferates, but the discount on its substance is also rising. One of its recent published fruit, which also establishes that its ancestry well pre-dates its fashionability, is *The Mind of Adolf Hitler* (New York: Basic Books, 1972), the 1943 psychoanalytic construct produced by Dr. Walter C. Langer, brother of Harvard historian William L. Langer, the latter a power both in the wartime Office of Strategic Services (OSS), and its postwar child, the Central Intelligence Agency (CIA). This report was intended for psychological warfare use by the OSS, and is super-saturated with the jargon so dear to Freudian artificers.

This and studies such as that of Dr. Zeligs display the recognizable stigmata of liberal ideological fixations. Invidious psycho-history peaks when it concerns itself with persons who are despised and execrated; the most widely hailed and celebrated invariably involve personalities whom liberals abominate. The methodology follows a familiar path of assemblage of all the drippings of gossip, innocent, irrelevant or frivolous, malevolent and poisonous, related to the subject, turned over with a scattering of related facts in a multitude of ways but in such a manner that the view of the larger historical backdrop steadily recedes to the point of invisibility.

Liberals who salivate over such creations are most unhappy when the same techniques and formulas are applied to their heroes and political demigods. This was dramatically the case when the master, Sigmund Freud himself, teamed with diplomat William C. Bullitt to fashion the psycho-historical dissection of Pres. Woodrow Wilson, which, like Dr. Langer's study of Hitler, also was published long after it had been completed. Liberal rage at Freud's and Bullitt's *Thomas Woodrow Wilson: A Psychological Study* (London: Weidenfeld and Nicolson, 1967), produced memorable emotional tremors. (Freud's dismally low opinion of Pres. Wilson was a matter of record well before he finished his collaboration with Bullitt in 1939. In the *New Republic* for May 19, 1941 (p. 694), Max Eastman reported that Freud had declared to him in Vienna in 1926, "Your Woodrow Wilson was the silliest fool of the century, and he was also probably one of the biggest criminals—unconsciously, I am quite sure.")]

[37]*New York Times*, October 9, 1948, p. 5. Mrs. D'Aquino was unable to obtain bail, and though not jailed once more, was confined in custody.

[38]*New York Times*, January 4, 1949, p. 14.

[39]See also *New York Times*, July 6, 1949, p. 16.

[40][It was thought that the prosecution was influenced by a previous treason trial, in Los Angeles, of one Tomoya Kawakita, at which time the jurors which held out the longest against conviction were three 'minority' persons. De Wolfe was an observer at that trial. JACL, *Iva Toguri*, p. 15.]

[41]*New York Times*, March 15, 1949, p. 18. See note 108.

[42]In addition to the first class air fare and allowance for subsistence for its flown-in witnesses, and $3,500 spent in behalf of the defense for obtaining depositions in Japan, there was a $12-a-day expenditure on the other witnesses, plus 7¢-a-mile transportation costs paid for every person who had to drive to the trial, and $100 a day spent on the judge, jury and court

attaches, as well as extra fees paid to radio technicians for wiring courthouse rooms so that radio recordings could be played and heard. One needs to have some idea of wage and price levels and the value of the dollar a generation ago to appreciate the significance of these perquisites. On the other aspects of court costs in the 'Tokyo Rose' trial see *Pacific Citizen*, July 9, 1949. (All citations from this newspaper relating to the trial were reprinted in the issue for December 21-28, 1973.)

[43]A defense maneuver at the start of the trial by Atty. Collins to facilitate a future appeal was an attempt to get on the record the assertion that the defendant by marrying a Portuguese citizen no longer was under American jurisdiction. New York *Times*, July 6, 1949, p. 16; *Pacific Citizen*, July 9, 1949.

[44]Richard J. Eisenhart. See New York *Times*, July 7, 1949, p. 14.

[45]On the Ikeda-Tsuneishi testimony, see New York *Times*, July 9, 1949, p. 2; July 12, 1949, p. 2; July 13, 1949, p. 11; July 14, 1949, p. 16; *Pacific Citizen*, July 16, 1949. A defense witness, Mark L. Streeter, tried to create a diversion by accusing Tsuneishi with being a 'war criminal' on the grounds of having maltreated prisoners of war, but the court sidetracked this. At one time during his cross-examination of Tsuneishi, Collins questioned him about eight regular staff announcers on Radio Tokyo, all women, and some of them Nisei, as was Mrs. D'Aquino, along with three additional women announcers who had worked for Radio Tokyo. Tsuneishi admitted knowing some of them. [Tsuneishi did pinpoint 13 Asian radio stations outside of Japan which employed English-speaking women broadcasters: Arai, Bandung, Bangkok; Hsinking, Nanking and Shanghai, in China; Manila, Rangoon, Saigon, Singapore, Soerabaja (Surabaya), in Java, and also stations in Formosa (Taiwan) and Korea. JACL, *Iva Toguri*, p. 17.]

[46]It does not appear Mrs. D'Aquino was ever paid for the interview given to Lee and Brundidge, nor did the latter pay Leslie Nakashima the $500 they promised him to help them find 'Tokyo Rose.'

[47]On Lee's testimony see New York *Times*, July 15, 1949, p. 12; July 16, 1949, p. 15; *Pacific Citizen*, July 16, 1949. Lee was the first to testify that the defendant had told him she had made the fateful Leyte Gulf statement.

[48]For extensive details on the backgrounds of Oki and Mitsushio, and for the latter's admission to memorizing the indictment, see *Pacific Citizen*, July 23, 1949.

[49]See Oki and Mitsushio testimony in New York *Times*, July 19, 1949, p. 14; July 20, 1949, p. 12; July 22, 1949, p. 7.

[50]On above see *Pacific Citizen*, August 13, 1949.

[51]Jordan, "The Trial of 'Tokyo Rose,'" *Pacific Citizen*, December 21-28, 1973, p. A-2. At the conclusion of Mrs. D'Aquino's testimony on September 9, 1949, Atty. Tamba introduced documents and testimony which demonstrated that Oki and Mitsushio had contradicted in court earlier testimony they had given to him in Japan, when he had sought their depositions for the defense. On that occasion, Tamba said the two men, who now had testified as to witnessing overt acts by the defendant, had told him she had never made any broadcast about the U.S. loss of ships, that when shown a copy of the indictment, declared they knew nothing about such charges, and that they knew nothing as to the identity of a 'Tokyo Rose.' (*Pacific Citizen*, September 17, 1949). For contradicting in court his previous depositions to the FBI, Norman Reyes was judged an unreliable witness and his testimony all disallowed. But the same standard was not applied to Oki and Mitsushio, who preceded him.

[On Monday, March 22, 1976 the Chicago *Tribune* published the first of two dispatches from its Far East correspondent, Ronald Yates, in which he reported having interviewed both Oki, now 63 years old, and Mitsushio, 71, Tokyo residents and "successful businessmen." Yates stated that one of the two admitted his testimomy against Iva Toguri was "untrue," though not identifying which one. He was further quoted as having said that he wished he had "the opportunity to talk with Iva and tell her why we had to do it."

The unnamed person, either Oki or Mitsushio, the two witnesses who were responsible for her conviction, remarked morosely to Yates, "U.S. Occupation Army police came and told me I had no choice but to testify against Iva, or else. Then, after I was flown to San Francisco for the trial along with other government witnesses, *we were told what to say and what not to say two hours every morning for a month before the trial started."* (Emphasis added.)

Yates' story quoted several witnesses without naming them, the gist of their admissions being that they testified as they did as the result of FBI threats to "do what we were told." Much of this corroborated suspicions of Atty. Tamba and others in 1949 that Oki and Mitsushio were intimidated by government agents under the possibility of also being tried as traitors. Though both had changed their nationality under Japanese law, they had not renounced their U.S. citizenship before an American consul in Japan, which left them technically U.S. citizens, and in American eyes, as such subject to treason proceedings. As Yates quoted his unidentified Nisei interviewee, "We were told that if we didn't cooperate, Uncle Sam might arrange a trial for us too." "So we 'cooperated' and we did what we were told and now many of us have guilty consciences because of it."

Most of Yates' report was devoted to statements by Teruo Ozasa, Utah-born, and now assistant to the secretary-general of the Asian Broadcasting Union. Ozasa, now 54, was the sound engineer for the Zero Hour on which Iva Toguri worked, and was in the studio for about 80% of the time she was on the air. In 1949 he had testified in her behalf via a deposition. Said Ozasa, "A lot of people who testified against Iva did it to save their own necks."]

[52]New York *Times*, July 22, 1949, p. 7.

[53]For Tillman's testimony on this interview see New York *Times*, July 26, 1949, p. 18; *Pacific Citizen*, July 30, 1949. Tillman confirmed Mrs. D'Aquino's cooperation with prisoners of war. Tillman's 1946 report detailed the bungling of her passport application by the American consulate in Japan and the similar botchery of her clearance papers from the Japanese finance ministry, which made it impossible for her to catch the NYK ship which left Japan on December 2, 1941. Prosecutor De Wolfe read the entire report to the jury on July 25, 1949. According to the Tillman report, Mrs. D'Aquino declared that she had been approached first by Mitsushio to take a voice test for possible employment on the new Zero Hour program then being structured.

[54]Tillman was under cross-examination by Collins for three days. He stated that he had been an FBI agent for 15 years and that he had conducted about 100 such interrogations as that of Mrs. D'Aquino. It was Tillman and another FBI agent, Dunn, who also interrogated Reyes and obtained the statement from him which Reyes contradicted on the stand at the trial; see note 67. On Tillman's testimony admitting the Yagi perjury/bribery, see New York *Times*, July 28, 1949, p. 4; *Pacific Citizen*, July 30, 1949.

[55]On the testimony by Reitz, Page and Keeney, see the International News Service account in Colorado Springs *Gazette Telegraph*, July 26, 1949, p. 9A. The day before these men were on the stand, the defense tried to introduce into the record the official statement by the U.S. Justice Department in Japan in 1946 announcing their unwillingness to see the defendant prosecuted for treason. The prosecution objected and the judge sustained the objection, but he qualified this by suggesting that this statement might be entered by the defense at a later time, New York *Times*, July 27, 1949, p. 19; *Pacific Citizen*, July 30, 1949.

[56]The prosecution paraded a succession of ex-servicemen through the first two weeks of August, the fifth and sixth of the trial, who testified to hearing various statements by Mrs. D'Aquino on Radio Tokyo while they were at various stations in the Pacific in 1944 and 1945. It appeared to court reporters that it amounted to closing the holes in the Government's case until cross-examination by Atty. Collins began. At the conclusion of this, there were views expressed that the defense's position was even stronger. Most of the witnesses admitted what they heard might have been said by any of many girl broadcasters at Radio Tokyo. On some of this testimony see New York *Times*, July 30, 1949, p. 5; August 3, 1949, p. 12, and especially the lengthy reportage in the *Pacific Citizen* for August 6 and August 13, 1949.

[57]Monotsuka was one of three Radio Tokyo engineers testifying for the prosecution, the others being Yoshitoshi Tanabe and Shigeru Okamoto. Under Collins' cross-examination they tended to place on the record material which enhanced the contentions of the defense. See other technical details related by these men in *Pacific Citizen*, August 13, 1949.

[58][In recapitulating the situation on Radio Tokyo during the war for Chicago *Tribune* reporter Ronald Yates, the chief sound engineer on the Zero Hour program, Teruo Ozasa, declared that the program was on the air seven days a week, always was on the 6 p.m.-7 p.m. slot, and always followed the same format:

'6:00 p.m.—an emcee (master of ceremonies), usually Cousens, Ince or Reyes would come on the air and explain what was coming on that evening's show.
6:05 p.m.—10 to 15 minutes of news.
6:20—Iva's spot, usually 15 minutes of popular music.
6:35 p.m.—5 minutes of commentary, usually written and read by Cousens, Ince or Reyes, never by Iva.
6:40 p.m.—Semi-classical music played by another woman announcer.
6:55 p.m.—More news and if any time was left after that, then sometimes a short humorous skit, which Iva never participated in.' *Chicago Tribune*, March 23, 1976.

Not only did she not take part in the latter, the only segment of the Zero Hour which might conceivably be considered propaganda, but Ozasa stated that "10 or so" other women worked on the Zero Hour in Tokyo and that most of them substituted for Mrs. D'Aquino on various occasions.

Other testimony established that the program was extended a half hour later on.]

[59]The testimony by Gallagher and Mrs. Hagedorn took place during the defense's innings in court. Their declarations and those of several other SWLs are reproduced in *Pacific Citizen*, September 3, 1949. Not many Pacific coast listeners stayed awake long enough to hear the Zero Hour broadcasts, which were received there at 2 a.m. local time.

[60]On Jordan, see note 51.

[61]A lengthy report on the content of these recordings, including the titles of musical selections and performing artists, can be found in *Pacific Citizen*, August 6, 1949.

[62]One of the best examples of a prosecution witness who changed his position under cross-examination and ended up saying things in extenuation of the defense was Nakamura, a Canadian-born Nisei, who, like Mrs. D'Aquino, refused to take Japanese citizenship while in Japan during the war. On his testimony and trip to the trial, which apparently was far from being voluntary, see New York *Times*, August 9, 1949, p. 12; *Pacific Citizen*, August 13, 1949.

[63]New York *Times*, August 13, 1949, p. 4.

[64]Olshausen's plea for acquittal lasted two hours. New York *Times*, August 14, 1949, p. 33. On other aspects of the plea see *Pacific Citizen*, August 20, 1949.

[65]New York *Times*, August 19, 1949, p. 10; *Pacific Citizen*, August 20, 1949. Both Ince and Cousens broke down during interrogation, and it was noted that the defendant, described as 'wan' and 'thin-cheeked,' also cried during Cousens' testimony. [It is probable that Mrs. D'Aquino had not recovered from the severe bout she suffered with amoebic dysentery on board ship from Japan to San Francisco in September, 1948. She later related that she had suffered such loss of weight on the trip that "the skirt which fit my waist in Yokohama fit only my hips in San Francisco." Quoted by Carroll and Power, in San Francisco *Chronicle*, February 5, 1976, p. 4.]

[66][The first reaction in a nationally circulated newspaper to the opening of the JACL drive to get Iva Toguri a pardon early in 1976 was a long story in the *Wall Street Journal* by Edwin McDowell published on February 6 ("The Case of 'Tokyo Rose' "). It drew a response published in the same paper on February 23 from George S. Guysi of Oklahoma City, who had been the case officer of the Tokyo Metropolitan Counter Intelligence Corps detachment which had been in charge of investigating persons of citizenship in countries of the 'Allies' who had broadcast over Japanese radio during the war. Guysi had personally interrogated Major Cousens and Major Ince, collaborated with the Australian Field Security Service, and had even testified for the Australian government in its treason trial of Cousens, which the Australian government lost, though Guysi did not mention that in his letter.
Guysi corroborated that the facts published by the *WSJ*, which McDowell, though having interviewed Wayne Collins early in 1974, derived primarily from the JACL booklet *Iva Toguri* (see note 1), "were independently confirmed by the Counter Intelligence Corps." Guysi went on to say, "It was and is inconceivable to me that the United States would try Mrs. D'Aquino for treason without first trying others whose conduct was far more questionable in matters of degree," and that "It is incontroverted that there was no such thing as 'Tokyo Rose.' "]

[67]Judge Roche ruled that Reyes, by offering contradictory testimony, was an unreliable witness, and threw out all his contributions, oral and written.
[There was an interesting followup in the Honolulu *Star-Bulletin & Advertiser* for June 27, 28 and 29, 1976 in which reporter Peter Rosegg published a lengthy interview with Reyes, today an assistant vice president of the First Hawaiian Bank and a resident of Honolulu since 1962, as well as a newscaster on both radio and television in Hawaii. Reyes still supported his position in his 4-day ordeal before the court in 1949, and remarked, "I wish I had been smarter then. I should have been much more direct and repudiated the statement I made to the FBI. I should have said it was a lie and proceeded to tell the truth." Reyes also re-confirmed that Iva Toguri had always read from scripts prepared by himself, Cousens and Ince. Reyes was quoted as commenting, "I have thought long and hard for many years and I can see no reason for them to single out Iva for prosecution"; "I have always believed she was innocent and unjustly convicted."]

[68][Reyes also was interviewed by Brundidge while at Vanderbilt, and Reyes' remarks were twisted in such a way that Brundidge quoted Reyes as saying he was delighted to do propaganda for the Japanese. See Reyes' comment on Brundidge in Honolulu *Star-Bulletin & Advertiser*, June 29, 1976, p. A-4. Brundidge was not well-liked by his fellow journalists, and had the reputation for "shading the truth," as Carroll and Power put it in the first of their two-part story on the inception of the " 'Tokyo Rose' Myth," in the San Francisco *Chronicle*, February 5 and 6, 1976.]

[69]New York *Times*, August 30, 1949, p. 12.

[70]D'Aquino asserted that her public acclaim of an American naval victory (battle of Coral Sea) cost her her job at the Domei news agency. New York *Times*, September 7, 1949, p. 10; *Pacific Citizen*, September 10, 1949. He also testified to having seen and heard her broadcast almost every day from December, 1943 until the fall of 1944, from which time he witnessed her performance on an average of once a week. D'Aquino's relation of the tangled status of her nationality after her arrest was instructive: she was arrested as an American citizen, treated as a Japanese while incarcerated in Sugamo prison, and

subsequently considered a Portuguese national when issued a ration card during the American occupation.

The U.S. Government in substance broke up the D'Aquinos' marriage. D'Aquino was made to sign a paper to the effect that he would leave the U.S. and never return. [This occurred in Seattle shortly after his arrival from Japan by ship to testify in his wife's trial. He was kept in jail for two days, under suspicion of being an 'illegal immigrant,' before signing the paper. D'Aquino, now 54 and a copy editor for a Tokyo English language newspaper, restated his views in 1949 concerning his wife's innocence recently when interviewed by the Chicago *Tribune*'s Far East correspondent, Ronald Yates, as well as supporting the views of others involved in the 1949 trial as to the real reason for his wife's conviction; "The problem was that a lot of the Japanese-Americans who worked with Iva at Radio Tokyo perjured themselves at her trial to save their own skins. They told lies because they were either bribed or threatened to do so by the American authorities." Chicago *Tribune*, March 23, 1976, Tempo section, pp. 1, 3.]

[71]New York *Times*, September 8, 1949, p. 32; September 9, 1949, p. 12; September 10, 1949, p. 5; *Pacific Citizen*, September 10, 1949; Associated Press summary of defendant's testimony, in Colorado Springs *Gazette Telegraph*, September 9, 1949, p. 15.

[72]Associated Press summary, Colorado Springs *Gazette Telegraph*, September 7, 1949, p. 20. Prior to this there were other depositions filed along such lines, one Tasuo Okada testifying that Mrs. D'Aquino had made repeated predictions of Japan's coming defeat. New York *Times*, September 3, 1949, p. 6.

[73]Associated Press summary, Colorado Springs *Gazette Telegraph*, September 7, 1949, p. 20; *Pacific Citizen*, September 10, 1949. [Judge Roche disallowed Murayama's testimony, as well as that of one Suisei Matsui, director of a Japanese radio station in Java using English-speaking Indonesian women as announcers. JACL, *Iva Toguri*, p. 18.]

[74]Associated Press summary, Colorado Springs *Gazette Telegraph*, September 14, 1949, p. 12; *Pacific Citizen*, September 17, 1949. In the latter source the defendant's experience was described as 'three days of scathing cross-examination,' and she was seen to have admitted having been involved as charged in the first three of the eight charges against her. But these were vague and pointless ramblings which simply sought to establish that she had agreed to take employment with the Broadcasting Corporation of Japan, on which counts she was eventually found innocent.

[75]New York *Times*, September 22, 1949, p. 15; *Pacific Citizen*, September 24, 1949. Olshausen in the final defense summation attacked the credibility of Oki and Mitsushio, who he said were "so scared" that they were willing to do anything to cultivate the good graces of the U.S. Occupation in Japan, including reversing their testimony to please the prosecution. See note 51.

[76]New York *Times*, September 24, 1949, p. 6; *Pacific Citizen*, September 24, 1949.

[77]Quoted in Associated Press summary, in Colorado Springs *Gazette Telegraph*, September 30, 1949, p. 1. See also New York *Times*, September 30, 1949, pp. 1, 15.

[78]*Pacific Citizen*, October 1, 1949, which should also be consulted on the outcome of the trial along with sources cited above.

[Mann was interviewed by Jerry Carroll and Keith Power of the San Francisco *Chronicle* in February, 1976 when the Japanese American Citizens League drive in behalf of Iva Toguri D'Aquino began to draw national attention. On the 15th of that month Mann joined those urging that she be given a presidential pardon, and restated his views, unchanged since the trial ended in Sepember, 1949. Now 75 and in retirement in a Bay Area suburb, he once more insisted that her conviction had taken place because the deadlocked jury caved in to judicial pressure, and that he "instantly regretted" changing his position from innocent to guilty after learning that the reporters covering the trial with only one exception favored acquittal. Beginning at 11-1 for acquittal, the jury was still 9-3 for acquittal after four days of "bitter wrangling," as Mann described it, adding that the members were "weary and angry, anxious to end the affair and return to their families and jobs." He further revealed that he and two others continued to hold out for acquittal even after the scolding lecture from Judge Roche. As Carroll and Power wrote, "Asked if he regarded Judge Roche as, in effect, directing the all-white jury of six men and six women to return a guilty verdict, Mann replied: 'Yes, I think so.'" See Carroll and Power, " 'Tokyo Rose' Juror Urges a Pardon," San Francisco *Chronicle*, February 16, 1976, p. 1.

The Columbia Broadcasting System's television news show "Sixty Minutes" devoted a segment to the 'Tokyo Rose' case which was far more sympathetic than a short and outrageously distorted previous stint on the National Broadcasting Company's "Today" TV program. The former was viewed on June 20, 1976, and included a short interview with Mann by Morley Safer, at which time Mann declared, "There have been very few months after the trial that I did not think of her [Iva Toguri] and think she was not guilty. I am rather sorry I did not stick to my guns."]

[79]New York *Times*, September 27, 1949, p. 1.

80New York *Times*, September 28, 1949, p. 16; Associated Press summary, Colorado Springs *Gazette Telegraph*, September 28, 1949, p. 1. The jury had been deliberating 34½ hours by now, and according to the AP report, Judge Roche had urged them to take their time, to prevent a possible second, larger and more expensive trial.

81New York *Times*, September 29, 1949, p. 21; see also *Pacific Citizen*, October 1, 1949.

82[In view of the behavior of the jury in the 'Tokyo Rose' case, there are grounds for holding that the racial angle was exaggerated. The revelation that the members were overwhelmingly in favor of acquittal for most of the time of their deliberations, and that their reversal was mainly due to the nagging of the judge, anxious for a conviction, hardly suggests that what transpired was a matter of general 'white' bias against a Japanese defendant, no matter what the psychic overtones were in the community at large. It is more obvious that this instance is another example of a tendency which has long been around and which continues to accelerate: judicial bullying of juries.]

83Collins quoted by Jordan, "Trial of 'Tokyo Rose,' " *Pacific Citizen*, December 21-28, 1973, p. A-3. However, the appeals court later ignored the cumulative effect of the errors cited, maintaining in its myopic legalese that *no single one* of the succession of errors cited, and which were admitted to have taken place, was sufficiently serious to warrant a reversal of the.verdict. It thus placed its seal of approval upon a miscarriage of justice as long as it was achieved piecemeal over an extended period of time.

84New York *Times*, October 7, 1949, p. 1; *Pacific Citizen*, October 8, 1949, later source especially useful on the defense motions.

85International News Service story, published variously, e.g., in Colorado Springs *Gazette Telegraph*, August 29, 1949, p. 8. The worst distortion of justice in the Pacific 'war crimes' trials was undoubtedly that of General Yamashita; one should not miss the book on it by A. Frank Reel, *The Case of General Yamashita* (University of Chicago Press, 1949) and the survey of the entire sorry business by Richard H. Minear, *Victor's Justice* (Princeton University Press, 1971).

86[There are three main versions of the fateful Leyte Gulf battle commentary for which Iva Toguri D'Aquino was convicted. The above cited version was put on the record during the 11th week of the trial while De Wolfe was questioning the defendant and is reprinted from the report on the trial by the *Pacific Citizen*'s reporter, Marion O. Tajiri, in the December 21-28, 1973 issue, p. B-5. The version which witness Kenkichi Oki testified the defendant spoke read: "Now you fellows have lost all your ships. You really are orphans of the Pacific now. How do you think that you'll get home?" This consists of 24 words, and is reproduced in the source cited above, on p. A-8. On p. 20 of the JACL booklet *Iva Toguri* it reads: "Orphans of the Pacific. You really are orphans now. How will you get home, now that all your ships are sunk?" This is a 21-word version, and with changes in punctuation, also appears in the McDowell essay in the *Wall Street Journal*. The version published in the text of this essay was attested to by three witnesses, and it is the one which the defendant declared she heard Oki talk about to Reyes, though she was not sure whether it actually had been spoken in a broadcast, nor was she certain that Oki claimed as much. The 25-word version is also the one which was attributed to the defendant by the Associated Press wire story on the jury's decision published in the newspapers of September 30, 1949.]

87De Wolfe also delivered himself of the following assessment right after the announcement of the sentence: "The jury has found this unfortunate defendant has committed one of the most serious and heinous offenses known to the federal statutes. She has had a fair trial and been given all her legal and constitutional rights." Quoted in *Pacific Citizen*, October 8, 1949.

88Collins quoted in Associated Press story on conviction of Mrs. D'Aquino, Colorado Springs *Gazette Telegraph*, September 30, 1949, p. 1. Most regional newspapers back-paged the long trial but front-paged the conviction of the defendant.

89Collins was angry at the Japanese American Citizens League for their faint-hearted approach to the case and their failure to support him in his campaign to get Mrs. D'Aquino freed. He suggested that their acronym JACL stood for "jackal." However, the *Pacific Citizen* on August 9, 1974 carried an eloquent eulogy by David Ushio, the national executive director of the JACL, which said in part, "Seldom in history does there appear a person possessing the moral courage and finely-honed sense of justice comparable to Wayne Collins."

It has been argued that concerning reluctance of Japanese Americans to form defense committees or to engage in noticeable effort in behalf of Iva Toguri, either during the trial or for some time thereafter, the general feeling of insecurity in the American social order after the outrageous experience of the concentration camps of 1942-1946 was the most important factor. Lacking a vantage point from which to work and avoided even by the elements which traditionally supported civil rights and liberties, the circumstances were hardly conducive to organized political activity in her behalf. It is an argument which is not to be set aside lightly.

[90]Collins quoted by Holmstrom in *Christian Science Monitor*, August 18, 1973, p. 7.

[91]New York *Times*, October 8, 1949, p. 3; October 11, 1949, p. 20.

[92]Three days after Mrs. D'Aquino's trial began, Judith Coplon was convicted of espionage in the U.S.A. in behalf of Stalinist Russia. She was released on bail. International News Service story, Colorado Springs *Gazette Telegraph*, July 8, 1949, p. 5.

The prosecution of Iva Toguri D'Aquino took place at a time when the Cold War with Russia was beginning to take on its major outlines, and a separate category of treasonous proceedings was making its way into public attention. This caused many problems for those not agile enough politically to keep up with the changing international scenery, cartooned so satirically by George Orwell in his book *1984*. A new class of propagandist emerged which tried to exploit the situation, blending the imaginings of World War Two with the realities of the new dispensation, though they were quite dissimilar and non-comparable matters. This did not reach its logical peak until nearly 20 years later, at the height of the Vietnam War, and was best exemplified by the reaction to the sympathetic reports by Harrison Salisbury from Communist North Vietnam. Salisbury's previous pro-Stalinist output was not memorialized now, the circumstances under which some of it had been written being when government policy here favored, at least part of the time, the dissemination of such material. But again there was trotted out the incongruous comparison with World War Two; William Randolph Hearst, Jr., wrote that the Salisbury stories reminded him of the 'treasonable broadcasts' of 'Tokyo Rose' during the earlier war, even though it was highly unlikely that he had ever heard one of them. See Robert Sherrill, *Why They Call It Politics* (New York: Harcourt Brace Jovanovich, 1972), p. 249.

[93]New York *Times*, November 4, 1949, p. 16; November 16, 1949, p. 17.

[94]New York: Harcourt Brace, 1948, introduction, xvi.

[95]High, "The Liberals' War," in *The Nation*, June 14, 1941, pp. 691-693.

[96]Justice Douglas, acting as circuit justice of the Ninth Judicial District, also granted Mrs. D'Aquino release on bail which was set at $50,000 but this sum was too large for her friends and family to raise. New York *Times*, February 8, 1950, p. 18; [JACL, *Iva Toguri*, p. 20.]

[97]On the legal maneuvering from the time of her appeal to the barring of further review of the case by the U.S. Supreme Court, see New York *Times*, September 16, 1950, p. 10; March 17, 1951, p. 8; October 11, 1951, p. 18, November 11, 1951, p. 23; December 18, 1951, p. 5; April 29, 1952, p. 28; April 7, 1953, p. 9.

[98]Mrs. D'Aquino had not been entirely forgotten during her incarceration. A New York *Times* article earlier in the month announced her impending release, and an ex-serviceman even offered her a job on radio four days before she was freed. New York *Times*, January 5, 1956, p. 10; January 8, 1956, sec. IV, p. 2; January 24, 1956, p. 10.

[99]New York *Times*, January 28, 1956. The Immigration and Naturalization Service subsequently claimed she was deportable under a clause in the McCarran-Walter Immigration and Naturalization Act of 1952, but all concerned were understandably vague about this. It became obvious in short order that this was ex post facto.

[100]New York *Times*, January 29, 1956, p. 41.

[101]New York *Times*, January 30, 1956, p. 24.

[102]New York *Times*, January 31, 1956, p. 3.

[103]New York *Times*, February 16, 1956, p. 58.

[104]New York *Times*, March 14, 1956, p. 19.

[105]New York *Times*, April 13, 1956, p. 50.

[106]New York *Times*, April 27, 1956, p. 10.

[107]New York *Times*, July 11, 1958, p. 3.

[108]See Appendices C and D to JACL, *Iva Toguri*, pp. 27-28, which include parts of the letters of Tamba and Collins to Presidents Eisenhower and Johnson which accompanied the petitions. Tamba's letter detailed his exposure of the bribing of Yagi and Kodaira by Harry Brundidge in Japan. Collins described how FBI agents arrested Cousens and Parkyns upon their arrival at San Francisco Airport from Australia and attempted to cow them into agreeing not to testify in behalf of Mrs. D'Aquino, and the clever stratagem of the court requiring the defense to submit the names and addresses of the 43 witnesses in Japan whom they wanted to give depositions in behalf of the defendant. This information was then swiftly teletyped to the FBI agents in Japan by the Justice Department, following which, charged Collins, "FBI agent Fred Tillman accompanied by one or two M.P.'s [military police] called upon a majority of the witnesses and coerced them to sign statements containing a multitude of falsities." See notes 53 and 54.

[109]JACL, *Iva Toguri*, p. 21.

[110]New York *Times*, November 16, 1972, p. 36.

[111]JACL, *Iva Toguri*, p. 22. There is evidence that the failure to pay the fine at the outset was partially as a consequence of cooperating with the counsel of the defense attorneys as a device for keeping the case open.

[112]Appendix E, "National Japanese American Citizens League Resolution," JACL, *Iva Toguri*, p. 29.

[113]San Francisco *Examiner,* June 24, 1976, p. 8.

[114]Though it may be a popular conception that 'treason' is some relatively precise offense as circumscribed as murder or safe-cracking, for which some inflexible mandatory punishment is always inflicted, the extremely subjective nature of the former seems almost too obvious to draw comment or explanation. It may be from a surfeit of moving pictures that the notion derives that traitors are always shot or hanged, and that the case against a person charged with treasonous conduct is always as bare and obvious as portrayed in films and on television, the accused bursting with the impulse to confess guilt as charged by Authority, or portrayed as having aided the enemy of their homeland in a most simple-minded fashion. There appears to be little of this in the real world, and the enforcement of repression varies with the enemy and the circumstances surrounding the total situation.

The ferocity of the hatred inspired against Germany in World War Two led to traditional proceedings against those accused and convicted of working in its behalf, and to remarkably severe prison sentences in cases where capital punishment was not inflicted. But in the case of treasonous enterprise on the part of those whose loyalty accrued to Stalinist Russia there were fewer executions, milder sentences and as the Cold War ensued, the mutual exchange of captured spies drew attention away from treason almost entirely. One cannot miss the sharp difference in the treatment of Mildred Gillars, as against Judith Coplon, for instance. (Is there any real qualitative difference between one who leaves the land of his or her allegiance and goes abroad to work in behalf of an enemy in wartime, as against one who remains at home and simulates loyalty while performing espionage service in behalf of a different enemy?)

The British executed William Joyce, the celebrated "Lord Haw Haw" who spoke on German radio during World War Two. But they put no persons to death who leaked valuable atomic and other secrets to Russia, acts which endangered the future of the British Isles by several hundred magnitudes when compared with the taunts and jibes of Joyce on wartime German radio. And the American authorities did not even indict Americans who engaged in the most palpable of pro-communist propaganda from North Vietnam during the recently concluded war in Vietnam. Americans engaging in such broadcasts in behalf of Japan or Germany between 1941 and 1945 would have been fortunate to escape summary execution upon return to the USA.

A most instructive exercise in the examination of the slippery relative politics of treason is the comparison of the various editions of the work of Rebecca West (pseudonym of Cicily Isabel Fairfield). Especially noteworthy is the remarkable change in color and emphasis from the time she is execrating the few English subjects who went to Europe and produced propaganda for Germany in World War Two to the later extended and sobered analysis of the labors in behalf of Stalinist Russia performed by a dozen or more English subjects while deeply buried in prestigious and respected jobs within England itself, along with some attention to the related atomic-secrets spying and thefts for Stalin by those enjoying American citizenship during the same period. Especially enraging to her was the sustained and undeviating devotion of the Stalinist Britons and Americans regardless of the temporary nature of this or that wartime expediency; it was the British spy for the Soviet, Gordon Lonsdale (about whom Miss West is probably correct in concluding that he was really a Russian named Molody who had appropriated the papers and identification of a dead Canadian) who remarked in his book *Spy: Twenty Years in the Soviet Secret Service* (New York: Hawthorn Books, 1965, p. 52), that it was "the postwar settlement of Europe" "which after all was what the war was all about."

There is in her work no estimation and evaluation of those who performed treasonable acts in behalf of England or the USA (a substantial contingent) while nominally the citizens of other countries; in statecraft, from time immemorial, those who are considered traitors in one land are taken for granted or hailed as heroes in that to which they defected or to whom they transferred their loyalty. In the Orwellian world of 1941-1951 the swift and repeated turnaround of political ties and alliances produced a succession of wrenching traumas for people trying to keep their priorities in proper relationship. The psychological agony suffered by the new Anglo-American liberal establishment which took shape during this time can be best seen in Miss West's immaculately-written *The Meaning of Treason* (1945, 1946, 1947) and the uneasy reformulations in her *The New Meaning of Treason* (1964, 1966).

[115]The *Pacific Citizen* in its editorial "The Tyranny of a Legend" published July 2, 1949, three days before the trial of Iva Toguri D'Aquino began, correctly diagnosed the coming proceedings as the trial of a generalized legend and not of a specific person.

[70]

Years of Infamy

Years of Infamy

A FEATURE OF WORLD WAR II WHICH WENT FAR BEYOND the wartime innovations of the previous half-century was the mass population transfers and large-scale incarceration of whole classes of people along racial and ethnic lines and cultural distinctions. World War I had seen extensive internment camps for civilians (there are still readers of e.e.cummings' *The Enormous Room,* but who remembers Aladar Kuncz's *Black Monastery?*), though they did not rival the much larger and more conventional prisoner-of-war installations. But the imprisonment of civilians in the fray of 1939-1945 exceeded in scope anything ever before known. Thanks to an unremitting propaganda still in full cry 40 years after the fact, most have at least a passing acquaintance with the German concentration camps of 1933 and after, though they came to hold far, far fewer people than the much more numerous, older, and much larger ones operated by the Bolshevik-Stalinist regime in Russia. The population transfers were as spectacular, and more novel, both during and after the war, and remain an issue to this day (see especially such works as Alfred de Zayas' *Nemesis at Potsdam.*)

The fate of half a million Volga Germans and many other peoples at the hands of the Stalinist regime during wartime has been aired in a variety of studies, though the subject of Soviet concentration camps was effectively smothered by the generally red-sympathizing American literary establishment for a generation and a half, and only recently caved in as a consequence of the global attention it all received stemming from A. Solzhenitsyn's grim *Gulag Archipelago.* But until very recently, Americans preferred to be regaled with stories of unique and allegedly exclusive German malfeasance, as their preferred model for a hated and all-pervading police is the 1933-1945 German *Geheimstaatspolizei* (Gestapo), not the much more ferocious and efficient and now 60-year-old Soviet Communist police machine, encompassing the globe in its enterprises, by which standards the far more notorious German institution was little better than an American county of some size may sport.

It is always more comfortable to dwell upon the failings of others, and the more distant they are, the easier it is to feel superior about it all. For that reason, whatever it may know about sin abroad, the general populace in the USA in this day is only faintly aware of the American participation in the business of mass population roundups and incarceration on the sole basis of ethnic or racial origin. This event has caused much distress among a few of those who considered the impact of it in terms of historical and future legal consequences, let alone the somewhat more intangible effects of a psychological or psychic nature. The literature on the subject is already vast.

With this attenuated introduction we may proceed now to the matter at hand. Those who pay attention to TV credits as they roll past at the conclusion of shows, and who watched the Perry Como Show for eight years, may dimly recall one which read "Costumes by Michi." This is the professional name of Michiko Nishiura Weglyn, a Japanese-American woman of uncommon talents, brains and good looks (oool it on the 'sexist' catcalls, please.) One of the nation's best at what she does best, theatrical costume designing, Mrs. Weglyn took time out from her expertly-written works on costuming, and related matters pertaining to both professional and personal grooming, to write a historical work on the experience of the American Japanese who spent the time of the noble Liberals' War, 1941-1945, expelled from their homes, stripped of all but their most simple belongings, and herded into ten bleak concentration camps from the California desert to Arkansas, for the duration, all 120,000 of them locked up on a totality of evidence which, the anguished liberal legalist Eugene V. Rostow later admitted, would not have served to bring about a conviction for having stolen a dog.

Mrs. Weglyn's *Years of Infamy* (the original projected title was *Days of Infamy*, but apparently a reverential editor thought it smacked too closely of reflection upon the adored departed master, FDR, who had employed the singular in describing the Japanese attack on Pearl Harbor), is a contribution to the growing literature on the American experience in operating such camps (in the exquisite hypocrisy of American bureaucracy, these have always been described as 'relocation centers'). A generation of works now streams behind us, beginning with the pioneer studies by the late Morton Grodzins and Louis Obed Renne, stretching on through other worthy labors by Anne Fisher, Allan Bosworth, Roger Daniels and half a dozen others of fairly recent vintage.

However, *Years of Infamy* is the first broad history (there have been several personal memoirs) by one who was actually among the incarcerated. Not only is it remarkably restrained (one sees almost nothing of this sort in the inflammatory works by those who spent some time in the European concentration camps) but it incorporates work based on sources not used by previous writers. (On the over 50 works on the subject so far the reader is directed to Raymond Okamura's impressive bibliographical essay in *Counterpoint: Perspectives on Asian America* [1976].

The situation, boiled down to its essential, the plausible excuse for it all, concerned the likely behavior of the Pacific Coast's Japanese ethnics once war between the USA and Japan became a reality on Dec. 7, 1941. The panic and hysteria prevailing in the area from the Mexican border to Alaska cannot be adequately described today. There were elements so unhinged by the Pearl Harbor bombing that they readily accepted the idea that a Japanese invasion of the Coast was likely to occur momentarily, and that the entire area to the Continental Divide should be abandoned and that a last-ditch stand be made against the Japanese somewhere in the mountains west of Denver. In general the fear of the next stages of the war with Japan was nowhere near that extreme, but it ballooned apprehension about the probable behavior of the resident Japanese in America, regardless of place of birth. Thereupon there grew the notion which led to the psychological support for the eventual expulsion of the entire Japanese populace from their Pacific Coast homes and their separation from $400 million worth of hard-earned property, and to be subsequently 'relocated' in the miserable camps stretching from the California high desert to the extremities of the High Plains: the expectation that they would act as a supporting force to the coming Japanese invasion, among the most agitated, or become an internal element devoted to sabotage and other interference and hindrance to the armed forces and the "war effort," was the comfortable rationalization for it.

Perhaps part of this sentiment could be traced to those who had watched the civilian populaces of Europe since late 1939, which gleefully mixed it up with the armed forces of Germany, in particular, in total contempt for the condemnation of such practices by the Hague Rules of Land Warfare. It was the New Warfare introduced by the Communist regimes of Russia and China, and continues to be a serious factor in world politics to this day.

The strangest part of this affair was that an exhaustive report had been filed by a State Department agent, Curtis B. Munson, after a period of secret surveillance, the gist of which was that there was not the faintest doubt but that the USA could depend upon the loyalty of the Japanese, citizens and non-citizens alike.

Nevertheless, the decision and program to uproot and incarcerate them all went ahead, seemingly motivated by the vague expectation that they *might* do something in the future, anyway. That they had yet not done anything at all did not seem to matter. The model seemed to be, unwittingly, a legal principle revived from the 15th century by the Germans in various regions they occupied in Europe, allowing for the imprisonment of persons in anticipation of them doing something hostile. Rafael Lemkin, the Polish-Jewish refugee lawyer who invented the ugly neologism 'genocide' in 1943, railed against the Germans for such a policy, but carefully ignored its American variant. The Germans undoubtedly had reasons for their variant of this precaution; the German General Staff charged that civilians committed around 4000 or so acts of sabotage *every day* against the German forces, and the Soviet functionary P. K. Ponomarenko boasted after the war that civilians had killed 500,000 German soldiers while fighting in 'resistance' outfits under Stalinist discipline. According to the Hague Rules, all these acts of sabotage and civilian killing of uniformed soldiers were 'war crimes.' But no American Japanese was ever convicted of sabotage or of killing any American soldier.

A major departure in *Years of Infamy* is a willingness to fix responsibility for the decision to destroy the Japanese-American community on the mainland (the Hawaiian-dwelling Japanese were only incidentally bothered) and lodge them in these incredibly desolate and dreary internment camps for nearly five years. There has always been a strong tendency to fog over and smudge the subject of responsibility, and to scatter it about in such a blurred manner that most readers have emerged from earlier works with the conclusion that it all just 'happened.' There did not seem to be much of anyone discernibly identified with the decisions which went into this political wartime trauma. Like Pearl Harbor, blame usually is assessed, if at all, upon a lower echelon of officials who obviously were carrying out orders from superiors, not inventing policy. For once we have in the case of Mrs. Weglyn's approach an effort to trace the decision-making process up the pipeline to the top. And the heartburn *that* has created among the surviving generation of affluent and powerful liberal inheritors of domestic and world influence and dominance has been extensive. This is evident from the tremulous and penitent introduction by James A. Michener down through the testimonials of a similar nature appended to the jacket of the first edition by the likes of Edwin O. Reischauer, Dore Schary, William Manchester and Carey McWilliams, all of which reinforce much of the earlier distress and agony of Rostow in his memorable *Harper's* article of September, 1945.

The preposterousness of this entire operation becomes more evident as time passes, and as it is examined by those not even born when it happened. The part played by the carefully nurtured war hysteria by the Roosevelt war administration propaganda machine has to be considered, as well as some idea of the nationwide campaign of Japanophobia which had never subsided in the interwar decades, and inflamed by the Pacific Coast press during that time.

Rounding up a racial community as distinctive as the Japanese was relatively easy. Not only were they plainly incapable of concealing their physiognomy; there were not very many of them, and they were almost all concentrated in one part of the mainland. (Left to the lay public, perhaps all other Asiatic minorities might have been included; Chinese played Japanese villain roles in wartime movies, and it was a rare viewer who might have been able to tell the difference.)

Of course, the Japanese were a very small fraction of the total of 'enemy aliens' in the USA and its possessions. Attorney General Francis Biddle estimated there were 1,100,000 in all, counting Puerto Rico and the Virgin Islands, when he directed them on Jan. 1, 1942 to surrender all their firearms to local police authorities by 11 p.m. Jan. 5. However, the sweeping order to round up the entire Japanese community later led to the inclusion of approximately 70,000 Japanese *who were American-born citizens,* not aliens at all. This made this aspect of the 'internal security' program of the Roosevelt regime quite distinct from anything else related to it. There were camps which housed small numbers of German and Italian aliens in the USA, contrary to most illusions about that part of the affair, but a roundup of all of them would have been a matter far too exhausting for the authorities. Not being racially distinct from the run of American white citizens, the effort to locate them without the aid of a vast organization of informers would never have made it. (Speaking of this subject, has it ever occurred to the reader how the Nazi authorities were able to establish who the Jews were in the areas of Europe under their control, and how many they missed?)

In one notable respect, Mrs. Weglyn does not flinch from direct attribution of the whole Japanese internment program to where it has always belonged: squarely on the doorstep of President Roosevelt. For once the standard liberal evasion of blaming it all on 'public opinion' in California, the Army colonel who wrote the executive order authorizing it, the Army general who administered it, and the entire category of diversionary figures which might divert attention from the White House, is bypassed. For once there is no irritating masking of the basic act. As Mrs. Weglyn bluntly puts it, "In short, Roosevelt's Executive Order 9066 — and the exclusion-internment program which grew out of it" — is where to start looking. This act she goes on to describe as "nothing less than a rash, deliberate violation of the Constitution."

The insistence that there be no more circuitous wheeling about the central fact was refreshing, though the ascription of the promulgation to 'racism' may be overdrawn. Roosevelt hardly held a position of superiority pretensions toward all Asiatics; few could match his Sinophile predilections, which was the positive side opposing his Japanophobia (John T. Flynn did a capable job of outlining the 19th century Roosevelt Chinese Connection). Nevertheless, it is long past the season when blurout-artists can wail that FDR was 'badly advised' about the program, and several other people are blamed for it all. Mrs. Weglyn has quite firmly closed the door on this ploy. It surely demolishes the limits of credulity for mouthpieces of executive puissance to maintain that the man at the head of a global war machine which saw him authorize the enrollment of 14,000,000 Americans into the armed forces, and stand at the head of an operation which spent in excess of $400,000,000,000 in the prosecution of that war, suddenly become so feeble, distracted and powerless as to be unable to prevent such a shameful and unnecessary caper as the Japanese-American incarceration adventure. The fact is that this program was directed as an integral auxiliary of the wartime administration's propaganda and its wartime encouragement of civilian sentiments as an adjunct to the firming of popular support for the war.

And where were all the pundits, including Walter Lippmann, and the big newspaper and radio mouthpieces, the fat, comfortable, affluent and prestigious, the war profiteers, and the looters of Japanese-American property, the big legal eagles and the professional liberal warriors, so quick to bellow in dismay at injustice abroad? Almost all squarely behind the administration's Japanese lockup program, approved almost unanimously by Congress in a voice vote maneuver, to disguise later pinpointing of personal positions. As usual, the sole voice criticizing the enabling legislation which put flesh on FDR's executive order was Sen. Robert A. Taft of Ohio, who called it "probably the sloppiest criminal law I have ever read or seen anywhere," though even Taft shrank from attacking the basic program, which he saw as one for the control of 'enemy aliens,' but fully aware of its capacity for injustice.

But the opportunities for hypocrisy were never all dissipated. Carey McWilliams, later editor of the liberal bible, *The Nation*, wrote piously upon witnessing a train of Japanese being shipped out to Tule Lake in the fall of 1943, that he wished the entire membership of one of the California 'nativist' organizations were there with him to witness the misery and anguish being caused these people. This writer also witnessed a trainload of Japanese expellees, departing from the Los Angeles Union Station in the late summer of 1942, while an employe of the Railway Express, and I would have liked as *my* fellow witnesses a lot of McWilliams' liberal buddies, who like the conservative patriots, were as wholly supportive of the expulsion.

There are several topics concerning this subject which receive special treatment at the hands of Mrs. Weglyn. Not only is the Munson Report and its total avoidance by officialdom properly memorialized for the first time; generous attention is given to the scratching and clawing among the State, War, Navy and Justice Departments to run the deportation/internment operation. Still another aspect finally given its proper attention is that which looked upon this mass apprehension of the American Japanese as a look-ahead hostage pool considering them as possible exchange bait for Caucasian Americans stranded in various Asiatic locations in the hands of the Imperial Japanese armed forces. And then there is the tale of involvement of a dozen Western Hemisphere states cooperating with the USA in also locking up their tiny number of Japanese subjects and aliens. Paraguay acted with alacrity and jailed their two Japanese, while Peru sent many of theirs to the USA for internment, which amounted to American jailing, not aliens of Imperial Japanese affiliation, but aliens of a friendly country! To such extent did the lunacy if not the pathological criminality of the program proceed.

As far as the personal domestic experience of the Japanese-Americans in those camps is involved, Mrs. Weglyn shows an almost monastic reserve in treating of it, and a detachment which is most remarkable, in view of her own presence in the camps as a teenager ripped up from life in California and deposited into the howling inferno of the southern Arizona desert wilds (the amenities so common there today did not exist there over 35 years ago, as I can testify from thousands of miles of railway travel back and forth across the entire area in 1942-1943.)

As far as the internal operation of the camps is concerned, there have been several memorable personal accounts. The outstanding contribution of this book in that regard is the solid chapter on the

Tule Lake camp and its many complicated ramifications, surely a monument to the extremes that native administrative bureaucratic mismanagement can go. The people responsible for that narrative could easily have made the transition to similar employment in Germany or Russia (or in France or England, for that matter, both expert in running World War II concentration camps,) given the opportunity. (It was Tule Lake which furnished the background for John Okada's bitter but memorable novel, *No-No Boy*.)

This is an expertly-turned work, even if here and there Mrs. Weglyn has employed flowery phrasing not customarily encountered in works of academic 'objectivity.' Especially appealing to this writer, fond of informative source notes, is the fund of elaboration in the documentation, as well as the file of revealing photocopied documents, lodged for some mysterious reason, not at the end of the text, but between the eighth and ninth chapters. Among them: Late in the summer of 1943, the bureaucracy created to run the camps, the "War Relocation Authority," adopted a program of selective release or "leave clearance," for some detainees. They were required to answer a fantastic questionnaire during their interview when it was sought to determine their acceptability for this leave of absence. My favorite is the following: "Can you furnish any proof that you have always been loyal to the United States?" Shades of *Fragebogen*, indeed.

My growing favorable disposition toward amateur historians, after a lengthy and sustained unhappiness with most of the professionals in Clio's lupanar, may have led to excessive appreciation of *Years of Infamy*. But I will consider that possible reservation when I see one of the guild of the *historikers* do a better job on this subject than has Michi Weglyn. And let no one who has never been hungry and friendless, yanked free from one's home and associations, for having done nothing at all, and abandoned to bake and dessicate in a sun-roasted and sandstorm-assaulted nightmare-nowhere, issue any smug disclaimers about the author's credentials for producing such a book at this.*

----

* [The capstone on the mountainous pyramid of hypocrisy which was the Roosevelt administration's policy toward the Americans of Japanese descent is represented by the 35 years of official silence maintained after the end of American involvement in the Pacific War, about the more than 5,000 men of Japanese ancestry

who took part on fronts thousands of miles in length with many units fighting in that war against Imperial Japan. The airtight suppression of information on this subject has recently been breached by the publication of the book *Yankee Samurai* (Detroit: Pettigrew Enterprises, 1979) by Joseph D. Harrington. (A substantial condensation of his book was first published in the *Pacific Citizen* for December 22-29, 1978, pp. 1, 54-57, 94.)

Though his concept of the political realities behind the titanic struggle in the Pacific, and his understanding of the meaning of its consequences, leaves a very great deal to be desired, Harrington's faithful pursuit of the details concerning the immense record of all these men, some of whom performed services which resulted in death in combat, while their relatives lay locked up in the U.S. mainland concentration camps stretched out from California to Arkansas, is a remarkable achievement. It also directs attention to the unfathomable split personality of a regime which could hold up the Japanese collectively to the U.S. home front as barely human, if that, and excite the most vicious and hostile propaganda against them on a racial basis, while secretly making generous use of the skills and talents of specific individuals among them in fighting against sometimes even members of their families in the armed forces of Imperial Japan.

How this was achieved as a psychological affair is quite imperfectly described in *Yankee Samurai,* but its importance lies in its author having cracked the tight wall of secrecy maintained for over a generation which prevented public knowledge about it ever having happened at all. It is quite likely, as Harrington admits, that he missed thousands of others, still in oblivion because of poor or deliberately botched record-keeping.]

Michiko Nishiura Weglyn

Where Was the General?

Some New Views and Contributions Relative to the Ongoing Mystery of Pearl Harbor*

General George C. Marshall

Where Was the General?

WE have been solemnly assured even in our own day that gossip is part of history. We find it from Thucydides to Tacitus; Suetonius' *History of the Twelve Caesars* is liberally seasoned with gossip. And some of the most graceful and elegant gossip ever committed to posterity is to be found in Plutarch.

Apparently it is an almost inescapable part of any episode which persists in remaining cloudy as to origins or content regardless of efforts to penetrate to the core of the affair by assemblage or analysis of facts. Perhaps there is more excuse for gossip in classical accounts, when the writing of such often took place many years after the events described, by which time some of the sources may have disappeared, and could not be examined. There is undoubtedly less excuse for it now. But we have events all the time which result in such circumstances, with any number of reasons prevailing to help explain either why there is a mystery, or why none should prevail.

The real burden of holding up under gossip bears most heavily upon those who wish to maintain sweet and innocent versions of the past which they dearly love, despite being faced by all manner of harsh and discordant facts which simply do not fit, and cannot be reconciled with the original or desired accounts. This is the predicament of all history which must deal in subsequent times with uncomfortable disclosures and discoveries, resulting either in the noticeable alteration of the original narratives, or subjecting them to deep suspicions and discount if they are able to withstand the uncomfortable heat of contradiction. And if this defense of official versions cannot come to terms with new facts or the uncovering of old ones, or discrepancies caused by lack of supporting documentary evidence, then gossip and its cousin rumor fills the space resulting from the failure of the upholders of prior rectitude to account for their inability to reinforce their credibility with anything but bluster, *ad hominem* criticism of their challengers, or the employment of devious and diversionary maneuvers intended to draw attention away from the problem. Like legal processes, history, when it cannot stand on documentary evidence, relapses and tries to make do by the substitution of testimony and opinion.

As we approach our own time, however, there are many complications which do not face those who are mainly concerned with the more distant past. One may write with relative ease of a time from which no one survives, and be guided only by respect for the sources, there being no one to issue heated challenges to one's product as a consequence of feeling injured by the account thus rendered. This state of affairs grows from residues of political significance which may still survive even if the events under question are many decades old. And the partisans of a person or policy surviving the demise of the actual participants become a veritable interest-group-industry in trying to perpetuate a memory and version more felicitous to their state of mind and well-being. Hence a clash is inevitable when those interested in the events, too, come upon the scene unencumbered by the emotional and political baggage which marks the position of the defenders of an established narrative. The case of the late General George C. Marshall and his connections with the drama of the Pearl Harbor attack of December 7, 1941 can hardly be surpassed as an example of this phenomenon.

Despite an immense volume of print which has been inspired and stimulated by the complicated events transpiring, we still do not know much of anything, and in some cases, nothing at all, concerning some of the actions or whereabouts of Gen. Marshall for most of the 24 hours which elapsed between roughly noon of Dec. 6 and the same hour on Dec. 7. This is of immense significance, since Gen. Marshall was Army Chief of Staff and as such directly in charge operationally over all Army affairs, which included the command at Pearl Harbor. This fact is at the center of the entire incident, and should be clearly emphasized at the outset, lest the usual muddiness prevail as to what the situation was. Percy Greaves, Jr., summarized the command situation in the following way in his expert chapter titled "The Pearl Harbor Investigations," in the symposium edited by Harry Elmer Barnes, *Perpetual War for Perpetual Peace* (Caldwell, Idaho: Caxton Printers, 1953), pp. 409-410:

> The Pacific Fleet was subject to orders of the Chief of Naval Operations [Adm. Harold R. Stark, in 1941] in Washington, *but, when it was in Pearl Harbor, the Army was charged with its protection.* The Hawaiian Army Commander [Lt. Gen. Walter C. Short] took orders directly only from the Chief of Staff [Gen. Marshall], the Secretary of War, [Henry L. Stimson], or the President of the United States [Franklin D. Roosevelt]. (Emphasis added.)

It will be seen, therefore, that the commander of the Pacific Fleet, which was based at Pearl Harbor beginning in April, 1940, and under Adm. Husband E. Kimmel beginning in January, 1941, had some defensive duties. But he and the Fleet were there largely to make ready *offensive* actions against the Japanese in the Pacific, in liaison with the Dutch and British navies in particular, as well as the naval forces of Australia, contingent upon various possible Japanese actions in this vast area.

All of this grew out of the very secret ("Rainbow") agreements which emerged from the joint strategy talks in Singapore, January-April, 1941. What Adm. Kimmel's *real* job with the Pacific Fleet was, in this context, was put on the record via the testimony of Adm. Richmond Kelley Turner before the board of inquiry conducted by Adm. Thomas C. Hart between mid-February and mid-June, 1944 (see Greaves, *Perpetual War*, pp. 421-422.) Knowledge of his duties undoubtedly played a big part in the official Navy Court of Inquiry (July-October, 1944) finding Adm. Kimmel innocent of any dereliction of duty during the events leading up to and through the attack of Dec. 7, 1941. (For an insight into how far political partisanship can go in covering up the truth, one should consult the observations on the infamous way in which the Roberts Commission went about its blackening of Adm. Kimmel, in the latter's own book on the entire business, *Admiral Kimmel's Story* [Chicago: Regnery, 1954], pp. 146-185. This should be supplemented by consulting the report of the interview with Adm. Kimmel by the Associated Press in December, 1966, published in varying length here and there about the country, *e.g.*, *Denver Post*, Dec. 7, 1966.)

Part of the difficulty in sorting out the various elements in the Pearl Harbor situation prior to the day of the attack stems from what may be called the "From Here to Eternity" syndrome, a reference to the famed moving picture of 1953, based on the novel of the same name by the late James Jones. This movie, now made much worse in a re-filming which reduces the pre-attack total scene in Hawaii to a monstrous soap opera, did much to induce the hazy ignorance as to what the situation was in the closing weeks of 1941. One gets from this much-shown picture that an aura of lazy unconcern with the world at war was the order of the day, and that the Navy was simply there for a casual vacation, while the Army was involved in even more trivial diversions. One absorbs the impression that all were there to indulge in sexual peccadillos and mild dissipation, with nothing on their minds except a succession of empty dinner parties for the officers and opportunities for drunken forays into Honolulu for the enlisted men.

However, since the picture dwelled mainly upon the empty distractions consuming the Army, and hardly involved the other services, lost entirely is the purpose of the Fleet being in Hawaii in the first place. There is not the faintest allusion to its preparation for likely attack on the Japanese, or even a single reference to the general situation in the Pacific. The casual atmosphere of scatterbrained lightheartedness allegedly prevailing there conveyed by this film helps to ingrain among its viewers a possible desired propagandist attitude, reinforcing the conviction that the eventual attack truly was totally unexpected, and unprepared for, thus sanctifying Roosevelt's pious "day of infamy" rhetoric, and rendering those exposed uninclined to consider any other view of the entire affair later on, when sobriety returned to temper hysteria. Moving pictures may be entertainment, but it is a rare one devoid of political messages.

That Adm. Kimmel was not empowered to engage in unilateral actions regardless of the situation, but had to await directions from Gen. Short, based on prior orders from Washington from either Stimson or Marshall, was already demonstrated in the case of the famous 'warning' to Hawaii purportedly emanating from Marshall (his name was appended to the message, at least) of November 27, 1941, in which Gen. Short was the addressee, with instructions further to establish liaison with the Navy, in effecting a *sabotage alert* at the combined Pearl Harbor facilities.

The Base had promptly been placed on such an alert, and there it remained to the moment of the bombing on the morning of December 7. (There has recently been a curious diversion related to this subject [see note 18 of the Pearl Harbor essay elsewhere in this work] growing out of the Burns Oral History Project at the University of Hawaii headed by Stuart Gerry Brown. In the transcripts of portions of Tapes #2, #5 and #6, former Gov. Burns seemed to recall that his informant on the upcoming attack on Pearl Harbor, Robert L. Shivers, the FBI's agent in charge in Honolulu, was supposed to have gone to the Pearl Harbor commanders with this information, though no evidence ever surfaced that he ever did, or even mentioned his special knowledge before the Roosevelt-handpicked whitewash Roberts Commission, before which he testified. Burns could not understand where Shivers got this information, though one might suspect that the Bureau may have acquired such intelligence in New York from their liaison work with British intelligence headed by Sir William Stephenson, who had full access to Purple "Magic" via their cracking of the analog of Purple, the German "Ultra" code. British possession of a Purple machine in London from January,

1941 on surely did not get in their way, either.) (One should consult William Stevenson, *A Man Called Intrepid* [New York: Harcourt, Brace Jovanovich, 1976] for a revelation of some of the interaction between American-based British intelligence and the FBI prior to U.S. formal involvement in World War II.)

This British connection was originally established by testimony of William F. Friedman, who headed the Army cryptanalytical team which first broke the Japanese Purple code in August, 1940, largely as a consequence of the work of Harry L. Clark, before the top-secret inquiries conducted by Col. (later Gen.) Carter W. Clarke for the War Department in September, 1944 (see Greaves, *Perpetual War*, p. 475.) However, in view of the chain of command prevailing, it does not seem that a visit by Shivers to either Adm. Kimmel or Gen. Short would have done much of anything other than stimulating a barrage of telephone calls and telegrams back and forth between Honolulu and Washington, with the Pearl Harbor commanders' superiors in the latter city becoming quietly hysterical over how Shivers and the FBI might have acquired such intelligence.)

We may now get on properly to an attempt to find the trail of Gen. Marshall, dividing the time span involved into three segments: 1) the afternoon of Dec. 6; 2) the evening of Dec. 6-7; 3) the morning of Dec. 7. Shortly after noon on the 6th there took place the interception of the so-called "pilot message" sent by the Japanese to their Washington embassy, announcing that a long communication, in 14 parts, was about to be sent to them, which was to be presented to the American Secretary of State the next day under conditions to be relayed later. A few moments after receiving this news, in his office in the old Munitions Building (the Pentagon did not exist in 1941), Gen. Marshall disappeared, and was not seen again until the following morning, at 9 a.m., 10 a.m., or around 11:30 a.m., depending on which testimony one wants to accept.

At the moment of learning of the 'pilot message,' asserted Captain Joseph J. Rochefort, chief of Naval Combat Intelligence at Pearl Harbor from June, 1941 on, and the key figure in the cracking of the Japanese naval code which led to the U.S. naval victory of the battle of Midway in the spring of 1942, Gen. Marshall, instead of disappearing, should have been on the scrambler telephone to Gen. Short in Honolulu. In a number of conversations with Capt. Rochefort in which this writer took part, in the mutual company of Dr. Harry Elmer Barnes, in the 1960s at Redondo Beach, Calif., it was asserted by Capt. Rochefort, though professing to be ignorant of the famous "Winds Execute" message of Dec. 4 wherein the Japanese had announced to their diplomatic people around the world a situation which could hardly be interpreted as anything but a coming declaration of war on the U.S., disguised in a false weather report, that he too was convinced that what was coming through the 6th was a sure prelude to a formal announcement of the breaking of diplomatic relations. And with Pearl Harbor still on a sabotage alert since Nov. 27, the Base was in grave danger if an *attack* were to follow, with aircraft and naval vessels still bunched up in various concentration points, in accordance with sabotage alert procedures. (That the aircraft carriers, heavy cruisers and submarines were not there at the time of the attack was a fortunate break.)

But Gen. Marshall executed one of the most famous disappearing acts in history instead. Testifying before the Joint Congressional Committee investigating the Pearl Harbor attack during the second week of December, 1945, Gen. Marshall declared under oath that he could not recall where he was the rest of Dec. 6 four years earlier, surely a day of major importance in his life. His memory was later 'refreshed' by his wife, Katharine Tupper Marshall, resulting in the conclusion that he had been with her, through the evening. Her engagement book, indicating they had not been anywhere else, presumably was the evidence, though, strangely enough, in her book *Together* (Atlanta: Tupper and Love, 1946), published the following year, she did not say that. She spoke of returning to their quarters at Fort Myer, Va., the evening of the 6th, but she did not say the General was with her, or was already there when she got home, or that he came in later in the evening. Nothing was said about his presence until she commented on him having breakfast with her the morning of the 7th, about which more later. Though Gen. Marshall's comments were confused, even with the support of his wife's engagement book, by default, there still is no positive statement on his part as to whether he was home or not.

Though all of Gen. Marshall's strongest contemporary supporters flinch from making this positive statement as to his whereabouts, also, this does not faze his very formidable hagiographer, Forrest C. Pogue, who, in Chapter 10 of Volume II of what has been emphasized as the only *official* Marshall biography (*George C. Marshall: Ordeal and Hope, 1939-1942;* New York: Viking, 1966), flatly declares the General was home all evening with his wife. He presents no evidence or citation for that declaration; we are supposed to take his word for it (*Ordeal and Hope*, p. 223).

For those who are not impressed with Pogue, and they exist, the absence of any solid documentary evidence of his whereabouts has led to the other areas which make up history: testimony and opinion. How much of this is plain gossip or speculation, regardless of point of origin, is unmeasurable, but durable.

Pogue,¡ the reverent curator of the George C. Marshall Research Library for years, and now Director of the Dwight D. Eisenhower Institute for Historical Research, from the small mountain of official papers over which he presides, has been unable, apparently, to find anything at all to substantiate where Gen. Marshall spent the time from shortly after noon on Dec. 6 to around 9 - 11 a.m. the next day. In the meantime, some have volunteered suggestions. There is one account which tries to place him at a dinner reunion of fellow graduates of the Virginia Military Institute. There have been those who have ruminated out loud that Gen. Marshall spent into the early morning hours of the 7th hiding somewhere in the White House under Pres. Roosevelt's protection. One long-held account maintained he spent Dec. 7 morning at the airport in Washington as part of the welcoming committee greeting the arrival of Maxim Litvinov, Stalin's new ambassador representing the Soviet Union, though this proved to be based on false information derived from a worshipful biography of Litvinov, later, by a specialist in Iranian art and a dogged admirer of the USSR, Arthur Upham Pope. There is still another, in an oral tradition among retired Army intelligence who are still too frightened to reveal their identity, who insist Gen. Marshall was a "closet dipsomaniac," and could not be found the evening of Dec. 6, 1941 because he was being treated for over-indulgence at the Walter Reed hospital, presumably masked by a false identity in the hospital admissions log.

Of course, there is not a shred of documentary evidence for any of these, but the persistence of a lack of explanation for the legendary mysterious absence of Gen. Marshall from all of normal channels of association and communication for a man that prominent has lent encouragement to those stories. For those who are devoted to the veneration of Important People, these are horrendous, unmentionable things even to think about, even though they are not yet punishable as offenses against "the officially established and sanctioned opinions of the State," shall we say, as are certain views in West Germany on various aspects of wartime history, 1939-1945. But they are perfectly valid "questions" to advance about someone else's heroes, in the time honored manner as a further example of the whose-ox-is-being-gored department. Perhaps this irreverence may have useful consequences in times to come. An audience ready to accept the recent accounts of the sexual adventures of both Pres. and Mrs. Franklin D. Roosevelt, let alone those of Pres. John F. Kennedy, may in due time come to terms with the revelation of the real whereabouts of Gen. George C. Marshall during the 24 hours preceding the Pearl Harbor attack, though this will obviously be something of a far different order than the matters mentioned above, if it ever takes place.

Shortly after Gen. Marshall vanished early Saturday afternoon, Dec. 6, the Japanese Memorandum #902 from Tokyo began to come in, and while the Japanese Embassy in Washington was busy taking it down, unknown to them, the American intelligence systems were doing the same, and converting it into English somewhat faster. And this had catastrophic consequences. The combined Army and Navy team of code-breakers were not only more successful than the Japanese Embassy people in coming up with an English language version of this memorandum, and well ahead of the latter. The difficulties of the Embassy decoders led to a delay in furnishing their diplomats with a version in time to make the scheduled presentation at the State Department, compounding their problem with accusations of planned deceit to cover the air attack on Hawaii as a consequence.

But this legend does not fit with the facts. Even the Japanese educator-historian Saburo Ienaga, though bitterly hostile to the Japanese regime which took Japan into war with the U.S.A., exonerates them of the almost universally-held notion in the U.S.A. that they had "planned a perfidious attack without any prior warning." This is "incorrect," Ienaga flatly declared. It was the Japanese government's clear intention to notify the State Department "immediately before the attack" at Pearl Harbor that diplomatic relations were considered broken, but this formal notice was delayed because "they had difficulty with the last long message from Tokyo." (Ienaga, *The Pacific War, 1931-1945.* New York: Pantheon Books, 1978, p. 136. This book was first published in Japanese language in Tokyo in 1968.)

Ladislas Farago in his *The Broken Seal* (New York: Random House, 1967), the most recent heavily-documented pro-Administration apologia and diversionary effort, frankly admitted it was the Japanese Embassy's inefficiency in failing to have the 14-part message in acceptable English in time for delivery to Sec. of State Cordell Hull, as originally promised, and not a part of some devilish "sneak attack" plot, though the latter misconception persists as the almost universal American belief.

What is really repelling about that drama in the offices of the State Department early in the afternoon of Dec. 7, 1941 was the fakery of Sec. Hull in pretending to read what was tendered him by the Japanese diplomats Nomura and Kurusu, and then launching into a diatribe of billingsgate aimed at these two, intended more for the record than anything else. Like everyone else privileged to read "Magic," Hull had already seen this message, thanks to the more speedy efforts of U.S. intelligence. Therefore, his whole performance was far more theater than it was the execution of his duties as a diplomat, and his simulated sense of outrage simply another contribution to the tight little scheme of propaganda being built around the entire incident by the Administration, to make themselves look like aggrieved innocent victims and the Japanese sinister, scheming deceivers. It worked in precisely that way, and the American public responded in a manner which must rank close to the top as an achievement of a propagandist's dream, probably unequalled in the history of devious statecraft.

Work on the Memorandum #902 was originally begun by Navy Communications Intelligence under the direction of Capt. Laurance F. Safford shortly after noon on the 6th, but the Army was eventually brought in to help out. This was no brief or routine communique. It went on for pages, amounting to well over 3000 words. Rather than being a catalog of "infamous falsehoods," as Sec. Hull raged, for public consumption, it was a sober and restrained summary of the Far East situation, from the Japanese point of view, and stating why they thought further attempts to negotiate the crisis in the Pacific were not worth continuing. Had Sec. Hull and his subordinates had to compose a similar memorandum, there are grave doubts that they could have come up with something less inflammatory in tone or more subdued in emphasis. It is significant that the U.S. public was not allowed to read the text of this fateful diplomatic paper at that time, which would have put to the test of critical appraisal whether or not it was a tissue of lies, as Hull succeeded in getting nearly all to believe, sight unseen. (What purports to be the entire memorandum, including the 14th part, received early Sunday a.m., the 7th, can be found in *The "Magic" Background of Pearl Harbor* [8 vols., Washington, D.C.: Department of Defense, U.S. Government Printing Office, 1977 , vol. IV Appendix, pp. A-130 — A-134.] This ponderous gathering of intelligence derived from the secret cracking of the Japanese "Purple" diplomatic code has finally been made available for students of the year before American entry into the Pacific War, but gives the appearance of having been well-laundered and bleached, or "sanitized," as the euphemism goes in document-verification circles.)

Memorandum #902 was decoded and in an English-language version ready for distribution around 9 p.m. the evening of Dec. 6. Now began the activities connected with its distribution. And Gen. Marshall enters the front row once more, as a prime receiver of a copy, but whom no one could locate in order to deliver it to him. Thirteen of the fourteen parts were in, and, according to Farago, the Navy delivered six copies, typed up on official Navy message forms, to Col. Rufus S. Bratton, Chief of Army Intelligence, Far East Section. According to the procedure in effect that week, it was the Navy's job to get "Magic" (translated copies of "Purple" code intercepts) to the President, among others, while the Army was entrusted with seeing that the Secretary of State and the Chief of Staff, among others, received copies.

At this point, the story splinters and nearly disintegrates. Col. Bratton told so many conflicting stories, some of them under oath before various Pearl Harbor investigations, that they cannot be clearly understood yet. Those he told off the record in subsequent times were even more puzzling. But the upshot of them all is that he failed to encounter Gen. Marshall at all, and it is unverified that he managed to deliver a copy to anyone even close to Gen. Marshall, despite claiming that he did so in delivering a copy to the Secretary of the General Staff, Col. (later Gen.) Walter Bedell Smith. Smith later filed an affidavit in 1945 denying that he had even been in the Munitions Building when Col. Bratton allegedly arrived there and purportedly left Gen. Marshall's copy for delivery to the General when he could be located. (Smith later was to become Chief of Staff himself, in the Eisenhower presidency.)

We do know, however, that Pres. Roosevelt[1] received a copy, and we are told that he shortly thereafter frantically tried to locate Admiral Stark, Chief of Naval Operations. Why he should have done that, if a warning to Pearl Harbor was on his mind, escapes understanding. Contacting Secretary of the Navy Frank Knox, Adm. Stark's superior, might have made more sense. However, warnings to Pearl Harbor were already stipulated as having to emanate from the office of the Chief of Staff, not the Chief of Naval Operations, keeping in mind that the protection of the Fleet and the Base was the Army's job, not the Navy's. Therefore, Pres. Roosevelt should have been looking for Gen. Marshall in great agitation, not Adm. Stark, or Gen. Marshall's superior, Sec. of War Henry L. Stimson, for sure. But we do not learn from any source that Pres. Roosevelt tried to locate Gen. Marshall anytime during the night of Dec. 6, and though it was plain from the context of the 13-part message in hand that a diplomatic rupture, at least, was soon to occur, no one lifted a finger at that moment to call or wire Gen. Short in Honolulu. In view of the above, it may seem to some that it might be more fundamental to ask where Sec. of War Stimson, Gen. Marshall's superior, was during the crisis of the night of Dec. 6, and why he was not enlisted in the effort to find Gen. Marshall, to tell him of the ominous context of this latest message, and have him direct Gen. Short, and through him, Adm. Kimmel, to reverse the sabotage alert under which the Base was operating, and replace it with an *attack* alert, which was the reverse, a wide dispersal of all important operational factors, especially planes and ships. Yet no one located Gen. Marshall all the rest of the night, either, even though Pogue tells us that an orderly was at Gen. Marshall's quarters "to take calls." In a succinct comment on the lapses of the Congressional investigation of Pearl Harbor, especially in neglecting to call at least *forty* important witnesses who could have added immensely to what we were to know about the entire event, Greaves *(Perpetual War,* p. 459) mentioned specifically this aide to Gen. Marshall, who presumably was on duty at least until 10 p.m. the night of Dec. 6, and might at least have been able to report if the General had arrived home by that time. (In later hearsay, Gen. Marshall was supposed to have been overheard telling Sen. Alben W. Barkley of the majority side of the Congressional Committee investigating the Pearl Harbor attack that he could not tell anyone where he had been the night of Dec. 6 because it would have got Pres. Roosevelt in trouble, meaning, presumably, the President's memory, Mr. Roosevelt having died seven months before the investigation hearings began.)

We now come to the early morning hours of Dec. 7, and the picture becomes a little more cloudy. In Mrs. Marshall's book *Together* (subtitled *Annals of an Army Wife)* she reported that the General had breakfast with her, eating from a tray at her bedside, she being indisposed as a result of breaking four ribs in an accident a few days before (the General is reported to have thought that she spent the entire day of Dec. 6 helping out at "an old-clothes sale," a rather wearying chore for someone with four broken ribs, it would seem.) She did not say anything about his whereabouts prior to the bedside breakfast. Pogue reports a different story on Marshall's breakfast, taken alone, and an hour later than usual, though both stories agree the General proceeded to go thereafter on his customary Sunday morning horseback ride, certainly one of the most fateful canters in history. We still have not been told the time this took place, and over the years we have been treated to two accounts of where it took place. The earliest generation of Administration apologists for Gen. Marshall's non-presence in his office Sunday morning, when everyone was allegedly looking for him, explained that he had been riding in Rock Creek Park, and those who knew nothing about this place were led to assume that it was so inaccessible that while there the General was virtually incommunicado. But that was soon blown away after the publication of the booklet *Pearl Harbor* (1946) by Charles Sweeny, one of the earliest skeptics over the entire Pearl fable. Sweeny pointed out that Rock Creek Park was really little more than "a narrow gully" running through "the heart of the residential district of Washington," and that it was only a half mile wide, with all its trails clearly visible from its ridges. A courier from the War Department could probably have contacted Gen. Marshall in a few minutes, using a motorcycle. But this account quietly shifted in later years, the ride then supposedly taking place on the Virginia side of the Potomac, and presumably occupying 50 minutes or more, according to the General's later recollections, as recorded by Pogue (*Ordeal and Hope*, p. 227).

It was followed by a return to quarters, a shower and dressing prior to the trip to the Munitions Building office. When did all this take place? It would seem that it would have had to have happened quite early. Though the Administration apologia had Gen. Marshall appearing at his office only at around 11:20 a.m., two other officers in sworn testimony declared they had seen him or were in his company in his office or that of someone else well before that time. Commander (later Adm.) Arthur N. McCollum, head of Naval Intelligence's Far Eastern desk, twice declared, once under oath, that the General, accompanied by an aide, had come to Adm. Stark's office around 9 a.m., and Col. (later Gen.) John R. Deane asserted he saw Gen. Marshall in the latter's office an hour later. However, the official legend rolls on, and in Pogue's masterpiece of official chronicling we find Gen. Marshall leisurely wandering on to the premises close to 11:30, a story dating back to the very first efforts at fabricating an innocent record for the Chief of Staff. By that time he was presumably the *last* of ten prominent political and military figures to read the Japanese Memorandum #902 *in toto,* something which Pogue thinks is almost commendatory (one may leave out here the possibility suggested by revisionists that Gen. Marshall's casual attitude toward this critically-important document, with its sophisticated implications of a state of war immediately impending, was due to his already having read it, or at least its first 13 parts, sometime in the previous evening.) Nevertheless, the tale told in the closing four pages of Pogue's chapter 10, "The Fatal Week," in *Ordeal and Hope*, is one of such unbelievable ignorance and innocence on the part of Gen. Marshall that one can conclude that perhaps it is a version of the past intended for a child's history of this grim and dramatic morning.

The picture that Pogue leaves with us, of a composed, almost diffident General Marshall, making his measured way about among several agitated, loud-speaking and near-hysteric subordinates and associates, is indeed charming, but the aspect involving his attitude of mystification as to the significance of the Japanese memorandum's content and further puzzlement over the import of the delivery-time of 1 p.m. at the State Department strikes especially hollow. If there was one man in the land who knew more of what the situation was all about than Gen. Marshall, it would be a prodigious task to pick him out. The direction of the Administration's entire drive since late July, 1941 was obvious to many who hardly knew anything about American statecraft, diplomacy and intelligence, let alone one who had total access to the entire substance of Japanese confidential discourse and planning. The circumstances of late morning, Dec. 7, 1941, were such that hardly anyone in Gen. Marshall's position would have labored and pondered more than a minute over the implications of this lengthy piece of "Magic" in his hands.

The insubstantial portrait of Gen. Marshall at this critical moment clashes in total contradiction with that revealed nearly a quarter of a century later by Robert Sherrod, who attained great prominence as a combat reporter in the Pacific War on a par with Clark Lee and Ernie Pyle. Sherrod, in his memoir in the symposium *I Can Tell It Now* (New York: Dutton, 1964)[2], disclosed a completely different Marshall, who called together a very secret meeting of seven trusted Washington correspondents early in the morning of Saturday, Nov. 15, 1941, just over three weeks before the attack on Hawaii. Gen. Marshall explained that his purpose in calling together this hush-hush seance was to tell the attendants that the U.S. was "on the brink of war with Japan," (this was a week and a half before Sec. of State Hull's brusque 'ultimatum'), and that America's position prior to it was "highly favorable," because "We know what they know about us, and they don't know that we know it," a roundabout way of telling the reporters the consequences of "Magic," but concealing from them that the Japanese diplomatic traffic divulged that they were vigorously seeking an accommodation with the U.S.A., and trying their best to escape involvement in a war with America. And Gen. Marshall further seemingly outlined to them Adm. Kimmel's real mission at Pearl Harbor by confiding to them that "We are preparing for an offensive war against Japan."

But when one reads Sherrod's account in its entirety, it reveals a Marshall so abysmally ignorant of the realities of Pacific geography that one may wonder what was going on in the War Plans Division under his trusted underling, Gen. Leonard T. Gerow. When questioned by one of his handpicked journalists as to what part the Navy was scheduled to play in this coming offensive war against Japan, Sherrod quoted Gen. Marshall as saying, " 'the grand strategy doesn't include the use of much naval force.' " Gen. Marshall, said Sherrod, stated that "he believed that our [the Army's] bombers could do the trick against Japan's Navy and Japan's cities 'without the use of our shipping.' " Were Sherrod not such a trusted member of the official reportage team and rewarded so many times for his faithful description of the war later on in harmony with official guidelines, one would be inclined to think he was out to make Marshall appear to be a simpleton. Nevertheless, Sherrod's "Secret Conference With General Marshall" (in *I Can Tell It Now*, pp. 41-42) described someone which makes one wonder a bit about who Forrest Pogue was limning on pages 228 to 231 of *Ordeal and Hope*.

But, as has been observed before, someone in his position with his knowledge of the total situation should have issued an attack alert both to Hawaii and the Philippines some 14 hours earlier, by the fastest means available. A rather feeble excuse in Gen. Marshall's behalf, that he eschewed the scrambler telephone on his desk because he did not want to run the risk of being intercepted by Japanese electronic surveillance, does not wash. There was no indication whatever that the Japanese had broken any American code (Marshall had boasted to the reporters about Japanese ignorance of American secrets three weeks before), and, furthermore, making recourse to commercial telegraph cable was certainly no better guarantee of confidentiality. The odds in favor of suspecting that RCA might already have been tapped were far higher than that the scrambler telephone ran such a risk. In any case, the real issue was the several thousands of American lives being jeopardized; new codes can always be structured. But Japanese discovery of defense precautions being taken in Hawaii would surely have led to the calling off of the attack.

In this matter it may be pertinent to inquire if Gen. Marshall violated Army regulations by failing to send such an important message by *multiple* means of transmission, in addition to waiting until the last moment. The one chosen, the slowest available, resulted in the ultimate in futility. There has long been a suspicion among people intimate with the Pearl Harbor affair that this action alone by Gen. Marshall was the tip-off that something extremely important was at stake, and that the incredible slowness in warning the Base was not just a happenstance.

The story from this point on has been told many times and does not need to be gone over exhaustively. The lethargic response to the Japanese message, with the additional intelligence that it would be presented to the Secretary of State at 1 p.m., and the final realization of the significance of that, and then the sending out of a 'warning' to Pearl Harbor, by the slowest method available short of homing pigeon, which arrived to Gen. Short after the attack had already concluded, is embalmed in our folklore.

A carefully-plotted-out excuse for Gen. Marshall has been expertly constructed over the years, though little of it holds up under criticism based on facts. Administration apologists have been able to produce an explanation for almost everything, especially the circumstances surrounding the sending of the last message to the Hawaiian command, circumstances which are far from clear and straightforward. In a re-examination of this it is clear that a large part of the total account demands another look, and a consideration of previously skimped, or ignored or avoided facts and implications.

It is acknowledged by Pogue and others that the famous 'warning' of Nov. 27 which ordered Gen. Short, in liaison with Adm. Kimmel, to put Pearl Harbor on a sabotage alert, was not prepared by Marshall at all, the General being in South Carolina observing Army maneuvers that day. Its authors were the Secretary of War, Stimson, and Gen. Gerow, Chief of the Army War Plans Division, who apparently was responsible for attaching Gen. Marshall's name to the message, for years assumed to be an authentic signature.

In later years, this message, and that of Dec. 7 also addressed to the Hawaiian Army commander, universally attributed to Gen. Marshall, attracted the critical attention of the famed Navy intelligence officer, Capt. Safford, a central figure in the controversies aroused over the 13-part and "East Wind Rain" Japanese intercepts. Capt. Safford became a student of serious insights into the Pearl Harbor story, and was the key figure in stimulating Adm. Kimmel in taking up his own vigorous defense after having been made the 'goat' of the Hawaii fiasco by the clever dissimulation of the cover-up diversionary artists working in behalf of whitewashing the Administration's favorites and pets.

It was Capt. Safford's firm view, after comparing the message of Nov. 27 with that of Dec. 7, that Gen. Marshall had not composed either of them. Utilizing the tools of internal criticism, he noted four separate particulars in which the two messages were al-most identical in composition, not to mention the vague and civil-ian-like construction of both, which he ascribed to Sec. of War Stimson.

In a long 15-page single-spaced typed memorandum which he wrote with Commander Charles C. Hiles, and distributed to a fair-ly wide circle of interested revisionist students in the late winter and early spring of 1963, accompanied by a copy of his letter to Dr. Barnes of Feb. 1, 1963, Capt. Safford scrutinized the two mes-sages in detail (Exhibits #36 and #61, respectively, as reproduced in the Joint Congressional Committee Proceedings of the Investi-gation of the Pearl Harbor Attack), the first from Part 14, p. 1393, a better copy of which was Exhibit #15 of the Clarke investi-gation hearings, Part 34, pages 182-183, and Part 15, page 1640.

The latter, the Dec. 7, 1941 message, was not the version previ-ously introduced, but was the *transmission* copy of the message, Capt. Safford emphasized, and that as Exhibit #61 it marked the only time he believed it ever appeared in the entire investigatory proceedings. He called attention to the clearly legible pencilled no-tations on the Clarke #15 photostatted version, which listed the times-and-places order of transmission, definitively listing Hawaii as fourth, and last, and not third (the official line), thus putting the location most likely to be struck by a sunrise attack last in order of notification. (1 p.m. Washington time was also about the same, Canal Zone time, the first notified, a very poor time for a sneak attack, while it was midnight, Manila time, the second noti-fied, utterly out of the question as far as a carrier-based aircraft at-tack was concerned. Why they took precedence over Honolulu, where it would be 7:30 a.m., an ideal time for such an attack that time of the year, was what aroused Capt. Safford's questioning of the adequacy of this "warning.")

In support of his contention that not only did Gen. Marshall have no part in the construction of the fateful war 'warning' of Dec. 7, 1941 but was not even on the premises housing his office when the message in question was filed for transmission in the War Department Signals Room, Capt. Safford called attention to the stumbling responses to questions by Major Edward C. French, in charge of the message Center, before the Clarke investigation on Sept. 28, 1944 (JCC Proceedings, Part 34, pp. 32-33.) The gist of this was that there was no proof Gen. Marshall was present when the efforts were made to get a legible copy of the 'warning' for telegraphic transmission.

The above material may be peripheral to the topic of this ex-tended commentary on the story which has grown around the whereabouts and activities of Gen. Marshall in the 24 hours prior to the Pearl Harbor attack, but that does not render it insignificant. And all such labors have been systematically minimized and defused over the years by official apologists skilled at creating diversionary obfuscation. Probably the best example of such is Roberta Wohlstetter's *Pearl Harbor* (Stanford, Calif.: Stanford University Press, 1962), ostensibly prepared, as Dr. Barnes suggested, with the assistance of the RAND Corporation think-tank and the presumable support of related networks of "mega-death intellectuals" fashionable 20 years ago.

In a somewhat different tactical exercise, this was also the fate of the "East Wind, Rain" Execute, in the course of which incredible efforts were undertaken to discredit repeated testimony even on the part of Admirals who testified under oath that it had been received by the Navy. Here the device was employed of getting their inferiors in rank to declare *they* had not seen the transmission copies. (The battery of people recruited to diminish the credibility of Captain Safford in this case was indeed a revelation. The shameful roundelay of witnesses changing their sworn testimony under the frantic pressure of armed service legal officers, ultimately leaving Capt. Safford alone in maintaining that a Winds Execute had been received Dec. 4 and translated copies widely circulated, is a very dismal story. The 14th and 15th chapters of George Morgenstern's *Pearl Harbor* [New York: Devin-Adair, 1947] is still the best account of this sad affair. The plain implication is that several higher-ups, with knowledge of this impending break in diplomatic relations between the Japanese Empire and the U.S.A., had violated their trust in failing to place American bases all over the world on an attack alert despite possession of this crucial information.)

In a further consideration in this exploratory commentary, is there any significance in the observation that, among retired principals involved in the Pearl Harbor business who later became engaged in revisionist investigations, almost all of them have been from the *Navy?* Admirals Standley, Kimmel, Theobald and Tolley, Commander Hiles, Captains Safford and Rochefort, and the expert testimony of Captain Alwyn Kramer and Admiral McCollum, stand out.

Nor should one omit from this group of retired Navy revisionists on Pearl Harbor the celebrated Admiral Harry E. Yarnell, who actually carried out a mock attack on Pearl Harbor uncannily similar to what the Japanese brought about, but some nine years earlier than they. In war games testing the Hawaii defenses, Adm. Yarnell, with a task force consisting of two aircraft carriers, four destroyers and 152 aircraft, launched an air assault 30 minutes before dawn on Sunday, Feb. 7, 1932 from sea about 60 miles from Oahu, coming in from the northeast, as did the Japanese Navy planes nine years later. The referees of the war games ruled that Adm. Yarnell's action caught the Base entirely by surprise, and theoretically sank every ship in the harbor and destroyed every Army warplane on the ground.

Adm. Yarnell was one of the very first and very enthusiastic reviewers of Morgenstern's *Pearl Harbor* and similarly commended the joint contributors to the *Perpetual War for Perpetual Peace* symposium, edited by Barnes. In a letter to Barnes, Dec. 16, 1953, Adm. Yarnell warmly congratulated them on their work, and said, "If the efforts of yourself and others could only succeed in your efforts to break down the Iron Curtain of dictated literature, it will do much to save our nation."

As against Navy busyness, there is no comparable output of publication, research and testimony from Army figures, despite occasional oblique contributions such as those by Gen. Douglas MacArthur's intelligence chief in the East Asian sector, Gen. Elliot R. Thorpe, and the strangely-unexploited commentary attributed to Gen. Clarke of May 4, 1961 in a widely circulated manuscript report by Professor Charles Callan Tansill, about which more later.

Could this preponderance of critics in one branch of the armed services have been an unconscious resentful response to the realization that the Navy had been unconscionably smeared with responsibility for the fiasco in Hawaii, via a process which had at the same time taken the Army, the real responsible entity for the safety and security of the Base, off the hook? Especially irritating must have been the extenuating circumstances found for excusing the top figures of the Administration, the War Department, including the Secretary, the Chief of Staff, his subordinates, and nearly everyone else related to them, while allowing Gen. Short to be thrown to the wolves as a diversion and a specious gesture of "objectivity" in spreading and allocating responsibility around a bit. The exception in this matter is of course the findings of the Army Pearl Harbor Board, whose deliberations began in July, 1944 and whose secret report was not made until after the end of the war in Europe in May, 1945. This report heavily involved the Secretary of State, Hull, the Chief of Staff, Gen. Marshall, and his War Plans head, Gen. Gerow, citing them for delinquency in failing to keep the Hawaiian command informed as to what was going on and, as Greaves put it (*Perpetual War*, p. 424), pointedly mentioning Gen. Marshall as responsible "for the fact that the Army was not prepared to defend the Fleet on the morning of December 7, 1941."

But the APHB noticeably omitted Gen. Marshall's superior from the list of responsibles neglectful of their duties: could it have been because Sec. of War Stimson had brought their investigation into existence in the first place, and making them loath and tender when it came to the subject of criticizing the man at the head of all of them? Though the central matter in this essay concerns those aspects of the Pearl Harbor subject related to Gen. Marshall, it becomes clear to almost anyone pursuing the literature surrounding the entire matter that the General's superior, Sec. Stimson, was an even more sacred cow when it came to pressing him for information. Sec. Stimson reportedly suffered a heart attack the day he was scheduled to testify before the congressional investigation, and did not recover until it was all over. He answered only in part the questions submitted to him in writing, and largely escaped the barrage of light and sound that was directed at all the main characters in the cast which took part in that fateful event.

Sec. Stimson, a sophisticated and veteran Japanophobe who gave away points in this department to no one, not even the implacable Stanley K. Hornbeck, of the Far East desk of the State Department, has been documented by several historians as an enthusiast for war in the Pacific against Japan even when he was Pres. Herbert C. Hoover's Secretary of State, leaving office early in 1933. His reappearance as Pres. Roosevelt's Secretary of War seven years later found him still of the same view.

And historian-apologists have been pushed to the limits of their abilities in explaining away that painful entry in his diary for Nov. 25, 1941, just two days before he sent out over Gen. Marshall's signature the famous sabotage alert to Hawaii with its mixture of 'dos' and 'don'ts' to Gen. Short (it was Capt. Safford's view that the 'dos' were Stimson's and the 'don'ts' were Gen. Gerow's, "like a duet in grand opera.") Whatever may be the truth, this famous diary entry, which became part of the public record which has stuck in the craw of every official apologist for the last 35 years, discussed a White House strategy meeting, and included the following: "The question was how we should maneuver them [the Japanese] into the position of firing the first shot without allowing too much danger to ourselves." As much paper and ink has been spent in trying to denature this remark and to mollify the quizzical as to its import, and to tell us what Sec. Stimson "really meant" here, as used to be expended by Marxian zealots trying to tell us what Marx "really meant" by various bits of his much more murky and tangled prose in one or another semi-intelligible book. (It was ironic that U.S. forces fired the first shot anyway, the Navy sinking a Japanese submarine at the entry to the Harbor well before the air attack came on the Base.)

A constant in the whitewash-blackout defense of Rooseveltian official history on the evolution of the attack on Pearl Harbor is the repeated categorical denial that there was any traffic among the armed forces, their civilian political chiefs, and the intelligence services, indicating that Hawaii was the prime, if not the *only* target in case war broke out between Japan and the U.S.A. Right down to the very hour of the bombing on Dec. 7, 1941 we find repeated statements in the defensive apologia that the attack was suspected as likely to be on half a dozen other places, even as distant as Borneo, but Pearl is pointedly left out as a locus for concern. A favorite distraction of the diversionists is the Philippines, though what American forces were there which might inhibit in any way the invasion of Southeast Asia which the Japanese were simultaneously conducting is indeed a dark secret. That the Philippine-based forces could not even defend themselves for more than a few weeks was shortly demonstrated, let alone cause much trouble for Japan south and west of there.[3] It was the American Fleet in Hawaii that represented the only assistance the European colonial powers could expect in their effort to retain their grip on Singapore, Malaysia, what is now known as Indonesia, and the former French colonies now known as Vietnam, Cambodia and Laos. But posing the Philippines as where the Administration expected an attack (precious little was done to frustrate one) distracts the inquisitive, and partially satisfies the hope that the latter will come to share the simulated surprise and conclude that this innocence pose is genuine.

In actuality, the strong possibility that the war might start with a Japanese assault on Pearl Harbor was a subject of heavy discourse, officially, in January and February, 1941. Navy Sec. Knox dispatched a four-page letter to Army Sec. Stimson on January 24, which became part of the record of the Roberts Commission investigating the attack, in December, 1941 — January, 1942. But few people have ever seen it or bothered to read it. This letter was entirely devoted, not to just a vague speculation on the possibility of attack *somewhere,* as one would gather from the preliminary remarks in Vol. 1 of the Defense Department's 1977 compilation, *The "Magic" Background of Pearl Harbor* (p. 1), but to a single topic, the likelihood of a bombing and torpedo plane attack on the U.S. Pacific Fleet while it was berthed at Pearl Harbor. Sec. Knox began by declaring that the "security of the U.S. Pacific Fleet while in Pearl Harbor" had been under consideration among the Navy for several weeks prior to his letter, long before

U.S. Ambassador Joseph Grew's much-publicized letter from Tokyo, also in January, 1941, suggesting a likely attack coming upon Hawaii.[4] Navy concern probably went back to the moving of the Fleet to Hawaii in mid-summer of 1940. Said Sec. Knox in the last sentence of his first paragraph,

> If war eventuates with Japan, it is believed easily possible that hostilities would be initiated by a surprise attack upon the Fleet or the Naval Base at Pearl Harbor.

Again it should be understood that Sec. Knox's long letter was devoted *in toto* to Pearl Harbor, not to Panama, Manila, the Presidio, Guam or Enderbury Island, and was responded to by Sec. Stimson on Feb. 7, 1941 in a 1½ page letter addressed to Sec. Knox, headed "Subject: Air Defense of Pearl Harbor, Hawaii." Like Sec. Knox's letter of Jan. 24, there was not a word devoted to any other place except Pearl Harbor. Copies of both letters reached Chief of Naval Operations Harold R. Stark, which he acknowledged Feb. 11, while Sec. Stimson declared at the end of his reply to Sec. Knox that copies of both letters were also going to the Commanding General in Hawaii. The presumption was that the Chief of Staff, Gen. Marshall, the Hawaiian Commander's superior, would also be a recipient, though this is not specified in the postcript notation concerning other designates of copies. But Sec. Stimson would hardly have deprived his immediate subordinate of documents of this importance.

Four days later (Feb. 15, 1941), a six-page confidential letter from Adm. Kimmel from his flagship, the *USS Pennsylvania,* under the heading address "Pearl Harbor, T.H." went out to nearly everyone possibly concerned with naval affairs in Hawaii, and also was exclusively devoted to a discussion of the problems involved in guarding against the possible sabotage of the Fleet, or its protection in case "That a declaration of war might be preceded by a surprise attack on ships in Pearl Harbor." The timing was too close to the Knox-Stimson exchange and the recognition of it by Adm. Stark to indicate anything but concordance and cooperation on Adm. Kimmel's part. (The Knox-Stimson correspondence of early 1941 and Adm. Kimmel's confidential letter to the Pacific Fleet are dealt with by Gordon Prange in his book *Tora! Tora! Tora!* [New York: McGraw-Hill, 1963], but in an obfuscatory manner. It might be pointed out that Joint Chiefs of Staff position papers throughout the 1920s and 1930s reveal repeated concern about a possible attack by Imperial Japan upon Pearl Harbor.)

It is in the light of the above, and because of the above, that Sec. Knox's 19-page double-spaced typewritten "Report by the Secretary of the Navy to the President" is such a sorry commentary, in effect suggesting the defensive neglect all around was so grave and encompassing, that one finds it hard to comprehend what he is trying to establish. Handed to Pres. Roosevelt personally by Sec. Knox the evening of Dec. 14, 1941 on his return from Hawaii (the President endorsed it in his own handwriting, "Given me by F.K. 10 p.m. Dec. 14 when he landed here from Hawaii"), the report on what had happened at Pearl a week earlier crawled with inaccuracies, especially in the parts dealing with non-combat aspects. One obvious concession was Sec. Knox's willingness to saddle the Navy with a large part of the blame, "due to a lack of a state of readiness against such an air attack by both branches of the service," a half-*non sequitur,* since this ignored the Army's primary responsibility for protecting the Fleet and the entire Base.

But what was immensely intriguing was Sec. Knox's declaration, also on the first page of his report, that a "message of warning" had been sent to Gen. Short from the War Department in Washington at midnight, Dec. 6, a warning which did not reach him, as he told Sec. Knox, until after even the warning sent under Gen. Marshall's signature around noon the following day. It would be of great interest to know who sent that warning from Washington at midnight, Dec. 6, and what it consisted of. Since no one could locate Gen. Marshall and since Col. Bratton testified that his superior, Gen. Sherman Miles of Army Intelligence, told him not to try to find him any longer after 11:30 p.m. that night, the sender of this warning must surely be a mysterious entity, if not ectoplasm. There is no account of anyone in authority in the War Department being awake at midnight, Dec. 6, 1941. No one credited Sec. Stimson with this action, and undoubtedly no subordinate of Gen. Marshall would have dared to do so without the General's permission. One may be induced to ruminate over whether this actually happened, or were both Gen. Short and Sec. Knox involved in a substantial error?

Sec. Knox seemed to be befuddled on the reason for the Hawaii Base being still on a sabotage alert, at the time of the attack, failing to recall that this was precisely what the two commanders had been ordered to do on Nov. 27, and had not been ordered to do anything different after that date. Another question comes up: why had not the men responsible for the defense of the Fleet and the Base, Sec. Stimson and Gen. Marshall, been sent to

Honolulu by the President to conduct an investigation? Sec. Knox should have been third in line, along with Adm. Stark, for such an assignment. However, his mission there alone, with the Army men not participating, further spread the impression, false but probably desired, that it was the Navy, which had sustained by far the largest part of the damage, which had been the delinquent in its protection, rather than the Army. This is how it worked out in terms of public relations and propaganda, and the traditional accounts to this day reflect this bias.

Knox, crediting Japanese espionage with informing their attacking forces of the precise location of the American ships, for obvious reasons did not give the slightest hint that American intelligence was well aware of this traffic via "Magic" intercepts for many months, though here he may have been in the dark himself as a result of the failure to communicate this "need-to-know" information to him. An examination of the majority of the actual copies of the "Magic" intercepts received ultimately by the Navy, though liberally covered with rubber stamps "Army," "Top Secret," "Ultra," and others, also reveals a rubber stamp legend, "Records of Naval Communications do not indicate transmittal of this specific information to authorities in Hawaii." One may conclude that, knowing Sec. Knox's reputation for integrity, this "specific information" never reached the Navy in Washington, either, and he simply did not know about all this.

To cap it all off, Sec. Knox omitted making the faintest reference to his four-page warning letter to Sec. Stimson early in 1941 of the need to develop a plan to defend Pearl Harbor specifically from a Japanese attack. And, of course, there is no indication of anyone's knowledge of the growing desperation in Japan as a result of the accelerating economic pinch caused by the global economic warfare against Japan by the Western colonial powers, also plainly discussed by the Japanese diplomatic service in the "Magic" intercepts of the late fall of 1941. (Especially pertinent here are the November, 1941 intercepts reproduced in Vol. IV Appendix of *The "Magic" Background of Pearl Harbor.*)

This aspect of the Pacific crisis is systematically neglected by the fuglemen of Anglo-American innocence, the increasing economic warfare carried on against the Japanese after the Roosevelt-Churchill meeting off Newfoundland in August, 1941. On October 23, the U.S. Commerce Department reported that Japanese raw material shortages had become so acute as a result of stepped-up curtailment that Japanese trade with a number of its biggest customers had virtually stopped, and that shipping to and trade with the U.S., the British Empire and the Netherlands East Indies had become almost "non-existent." (New York *Times*, October 24, 1941, p. 36). On December 1, the National Industrial Conference Board published a work titled "The Effects of the Allied Economic Blockade on Japan," in which it stated that normal Japanese imports of raw materials covering not only war supplies but necessities for the civilian population had been reduced by about 75%, and cited a report of the Chinese News Service that Japan was "on the verge of economic collapse." (New York *Times*, December 2, 1941, p. 6.) And in the *Congressional Record*, 77th Congress, Second Session, December 8, 1942, Rep. Jeanette Rankin of Montana, the only member of Congress who had refused to vote for a declaration of war on Japan the previous year on that date, remarked that near the same day as the NICB report on Japanese economic desperation was published the previous year, a "prominent non-Japanese Oriental" had told her that the situation in the Pacific was not only "serious," but that "Japan has no choice but to go to war or to submit to economic slavery for the rest of her existence." General information of this nature, if widely read and understood, might have made possible an appreciation of another reason for Pearl Harbor other than the simpleminded explanation fed into public discourse for the purpose of maximizing patriotic sentiments and nationalistic outrage and hatred.

The veteran reporter, political analyst and commentator for the New York *Times*, Arthur Krock, made a glancing remark in his memoirs (*Sixty Years on the Firing Lines*) about the "posse of apologists" who made a veritable industry out of "explaining away" all the disjointed irregularities in the Roosevelt Administration's conduct of affairs in the months prior to the Pearl Harbor bombing. In actuality, Krock's "posse" grew over the last 40 years to comprise a multitudinous constabulary. No defensive apologetic effort in American history has been so extensive or sustained as that which has sought to perfume Mr. Roosevelt and his eager-for-war regime, and how they eventually got it, while seeking to banish all criticism and suspicion of their role in this disaster.[5]

However, the more this industriousness in behalf of Administration purity and innocence branches out, the more tenacious grows the conviction that the total situation seen in the light of over 35 years of revelations, exposures and discoveries confirms the reverse, and the belief hardens that a gigantic camouflage diversion has taken place instead, succeeding in part at least in diverting attention from many basic disagreeable and distressing facts, while seeking to encourage favorable consideration of an evasive mollification.

As the people involved die (very few of the participants and principals in that great drama are still alive), and as the documents either vanish, one by one, or are declared never to have existed, there will tend to precipitate out a vague narrative steering its readers into accepting a genteel and respectable Establishment whitewash. But the anti-Establishment's counter-story will hardly give ground for that reason. The former's eyewash may appear to have won the day, if one considers the simple tales told the youth, to this time still nearly clean of any reconciliation with the contradictory material placed on the record by their adversaries, the revisionists. But it is unlikely that the latter will disappear or go away, or abandon the field, in the future. It is just as possible that the efforts to modify or demolish the Establishment monolith will be augmented instead. For there are many in close accord with the observations of Joseph D. Harrington, the author of *Yankee Samurai* (1979), who maintained that challenging the *official* accounts of *everything* was not only a "civic responsibility" but also "great fun."

A PERTINENT POSTCRIPT ON THE "WINDS" MESSAGE AFFAIR

When the Japanese Foreign Office sent out Circular #2353 Nov. 19, 1941, advising their embassy and consular people in Washington and presumably a number of other places in the world of the possible coming announcement of the suspension of diplomatic relations with any of three other countries, it was sent in Purple code, which they believed no one had deciphered. Early in December, the 1st and 2nd, all materials and machines connected with handling Purple were ordered destroyed. Therefore, when the decision was made to break relations and go to war with the U.S.A. on Dec. 4, the decision buried within a radio newscast disguised as a pre-arranged false weather report, the Foreign Office sent it out in Japanese Morse Code, which made its transmission and subsequent understanding quite simple to all. Believing that the confidential message informing intended recipients what HIGASHI NO KAZE AME would mean in this context was still a secret, its execution would therefore excite no suspicion among non-Japanese interceptors, while widespread dissemination, repeatedly, would guarantee that few if any of those for whom it was intended would miss it. The official American line is and has been that though Circular #2353 was intercepted, the "execute" was not.

The editors of the world-known Tokyo newspaper *Asahi Shimbun*, in their book *The Pacific Rivals* (New York: Weatherhill, 1972, p. 91), declare that the "Easterly wind, rain" message was "flashed repeatedly" at the direction of Foreign Minister Shigenori Togo. But the defenders of official innocence here have made a convention out of denying that it was received here no matter how often it was sent out, or that it was received in a garbled form which made it unintelligible, or that it was too ambiguous to be construed as a coded message indicating a definite decision of Japan to go to war with the U.S.A. Furthermore, if received, it could not have been of any real assistance to American intelligence because it had nothing to do with Pearl Harbor. This latter line apparently is based on the notion that the Winds Execute should have been accompanied by a map of the naval and military installations in Hawaii, in order to be taken seriously.

The smugness about and surefooted dismissal of this critical issue has especially characterized the approach of the Roosevelt defense squad since the publication of Mrs. Wohlstetter's book in 1962, and is reflected in the official publication of the "Magic" intercepts beginning in 1977 by the Defense Department, described above. This massive multi-volume work, weighing 20 pounds, escapes mention of the subject entirely, except for a repetition of a 1945 commentary which passed over the matter airily as of no consequence.

However, before we move on from the Winds Execute matter, one more contribution should be made to the subject which should shake the official diversion specialists and the "blackout" and "blurout" (to use Barnes' terms) exponents, and bring into focus again Capt. Safford's stubborn position on the reception and wide distribution of this message. What time has effected should make all the scoffers at Capt. Safford stand back a bit (even the would-be revisionist book on Pearl Harbor by Bruce R. Bartlett, *Cover-up: The Politics of Pearl Harbor, 1941-1946* [New Rochelle, N.Y.: Arlington House, 1978], contains a malicious sally at Capt. Safford in the manner of Pogue that would have done justice to the work of any "blackout boy," from the original old masters, Morison, Millis, Feis, Bailey, Perkins or Rauch, to any of the undistinguished non-entities of the current scene.)

On March 11, 1980 there was declassified and placed in the National Archives Document SRH-051, in Record Group 457, a "sanitized" version of a 17-page typewritten interview, January 13, 1977, conducted by Raymond Schmidt, a historian with the Naval Security Group (since reassigned to the National Security

Agency), with Ralph T. Briggs. Briggs, chief watch supervisor at the Naval Communications Station at Cheltenham, Maryland in December, 1941, related in detail his interception of the Winds Execute message the evening of Dec. 4.[6] He went on to relate his transmission of it to Naval Communications in Washington by teletype, the message also being delivered later by pouch. He also stated that he entered this interception of the false weather report, HIGASHI NO KAZE AME, in his log sheet of intercepted messages.

Briggs added the sensational information that this log sheet, presumed by all to have been destroyed sometime during the war, had survived, and that he had come across it himself between 1960 and 1962 while he was officer in charge of Naval World War II intelligence and "crypto" archives. He described his verification of the time of receipt on the log sheet, and said, "I then made a written entry on the upper right hand margin of this log sheet concerning the fact that I, as officer in charge, on the date in question, had sighted and verified that this was a recorded original entry of the Winds execute message."

Briggs then returned the log sheet to the files without making a copy, from which point it presumably went into Naval Security Group archives. It is believed that Briggs's log has been rediscovered by NSG, and that it is possible copies have been made available to favored personages, though others seeking it have been thus far stonewalled in their effort also to get access to it.

The puzzling aspect of all this is the silence of Capt. Safford for so many years on Briggs. It might be explained that Brigg's existence was known to revisionists as well since 1945-46, yet the failure of a single work on Pearl Harbor to mention even his name is fully as mystifying. Briggs relates in his interview with Dr. Schmidt that Capt. Safford had contacted him and that the possibility of his testifying before the Congressional investigation had been discussed by them four or five times. Briggs stated that he was not averse to this, but that he was eventually ordered by his superior at the Cheltenham installation, a Capt. John Harper, that he was not to testify, nor was he to continue meeting with Capt. Safford. (Briggs stated that Capt. Harper was very disturbed when he ordered him, Briggs, to remain silent about this subject; it would be most interesting to discover how far up the chain of command Capt. Harper's orders could be located.)

It is strange that no revisionist ever asked Capt. Safford where his operation, on Nebraska Avenue in Washington, got their copy of the raw intercept of the Winds Execute. They were not an intercept station, and obviously had to get it from someone. That Cheltenham had made the intercept was a matter of record among all, but how it got from there to Capt. Safford's team, and Capt. Alwyn Kramer, under whom the translated copies were prepared for distribution, was never explained by anyone. The Briggs interview furnishes us with this missing piece.

In a similar manner, the famed luncheon of May 4, 1961 involving Gen. Carter W. Clarke, Gen. Bonner Fellers and Prof. Tansill, during which other materials relating to Winds Execute were revealed, never became utilized by any writers of revisionist persuasion, then or later, even by Prof. Tansill himself. Though a 4-page single-spaced typed copy of Tansill's notes has circulated for nearly 20 years, it has not been employed in any context, to this writer's knowledge. Gen. Clarke, Deputy Chief of the Military Intelligence Service, was reported by Prof. Tansill to have declared that the Winds Execute was picked up also by the Coast and Geodetic Survey Station at Mobile, Alabama and sent on to Washington the following day.

The next move is up to the official defenders and the salvagers of prior legends of ignorance and innocence. But the publication of Ralph T. Briggs' January, 1977 interview and his December, 1941 message reception log should take place at the same time the next obfuscatory campaign is made to wrap up the Winds Execute in impenetrable diversionary irrelevance and historical bafflegab.

* * *

DOCUMENT

No. 148

From: Tokyo   November 19, 1941
To: Washington   Circular 2353

Regarding the broadcast of a special message in an emergency.

In case of emergency, (danger of cutting off our diplomatic relations), and the cutting off of international communications, the following warning will be added in the middle of the daily Japanese language short wave news broadcast.

(1)   In case of a Japan-U.S. relations in danger — HIGASHI NO KAZEAME (East Wind rain).

(2)   Japan-U.S.S.R. relations — KITANOKAZE KUMORI (North Wind cloudy).

(3)   Japan-British relations: NISHI NO KAZE HARE — (West Wind clear).

This signal will be given in the middle and at the end as a weather forecast and last sentence will be repeated twice. When this is heard please destroy all code papers, etc. This is as yet to be a completely secret arrangement.

Trans. 11-28-41

Above from p. A-81 of The "Magic" Background of Pearl Harbor, vol. IV Appendix (8 vols., Washington, D.C.: Department of Defense, 1977).

NOTES

*
IT IS not the purpose of this essay to try to condense in this much space the entire story of Pearl Harbor. This is a task which has e-luded more than a score of writers who have tried to do it in large books. The principal objective here is to concentrate on the drama of the ten days, and especially the last 24 hours, prior to the out-break of war between the U.S.A. and Japan following the attack of the latter on Hawaii December 7, 1941. It is intended to be read in conjunction with this writer's essay, "Pearl Harbor: Antece-dents, Background, and Consequences" (in *The Saga Of Hog Island and Other Essays in Inconvenient History* [Colorado Springs: Ralph Myles Publisher, 1977], pp. 114-131). The essay at hand was inspired as a follow-up to a single sentence in the former (9th line from bottom, p. 122), where something of the larger picture of U.S.A.-Japanese relations was one of the principal concerns.

The course and collapse of the diplomatic talks between the American and Japanese governments between September and late November, 1941 is the real backdrop of the account here narrated, with emphasis on what are new or previously unstressed aspects of the happenings from November 26 through December 7. Analysis of the fine points of the diplomatic presentations dealing with the Far Eastern situation is also of secondary consideration at this stage. Partisans of the rival positions may quarrel over the rightness or wrongness of them for a long time. But Americans had the up-per hand in these conversations, by dint of cracking the Japanese diplomatic code of highest priority, "Purple," having made it pos-sible to read their adversary's ideas and secrets while at the same time keeping theirs from Japanese scrutiny. The foundering of the talks over differences on China policy can be blamed as easily on the Roosevelt Administration as on the Japanese, even if neither side were ready to make any substantial concessions to the other on this specific point. But, in retrospect, what the Roosevelt parti-sans wanted in East Asia was never implemented, even after win-ning a war, and probably could never have been implemented, un-less it was preferred that there be a solidly-Communist Far East at the conclusion, which does not seem to have been expected by the short-view politicians. But such a possibility was plain to see prior to the war, and A Red East Asia was certainly no political improvement over a Japanese-dominated East Asia as it was in 1941. As the near-total destruction of the European colonial system in East Asia and the Pacific, the succoring of which was jointly a high Roosevelt original priority, also swiftly followed the immense Communist encroachment from 1945 onward, one can hardly look upon the "New Order" thereafter as something to take much pride in, and the later wars over real estate still in dispute from the Pacific War, in Korea and Viet Nam, have certainly added emphasis to this observation.

A thousand evasions of this political reality are possible and many of them have been paraded by us over the years, including the revival of such primitive ones as the bogus indignation over, and the necessity to destroy, the allegedly unequalled political sin of unique Japanese "militarism" (for the past 20 years our politicians and journalists have whined and stewed that the Japanese are lamentably too *anti*-militaristic). So the problem is an endemic one, and may be centuries in existence prior to satisfactory resolution, a matter deeply imbedded in our total situation. As good a statement as one is likely to find in so few words on the remaining difficulty is that of the late William L. Neumann:[‡]

> " 'Good patriot, bad historian,' a comment first made in regard to Poggio Bracciolini, author of *Eight Books of Florentine History*, can all too often be applied to modern historians as well. Enveloped in nationalism, that omnipresent malaise of the modern world, the scholar has made little progress toward his commonly proclaimed goal of objectivity when his subject has involved the interests of his own nation or its enemies."

[1] Lewis Carroll's fantasy character who suggested salutary consequences might follow in developing the ability to believe six impossible things before breakfast probably had an unconscious impact upon establishment official writers of Roosevelt Administration innocence in developing their version of the Pearl Harbor story. *In toto* they eventually gathered together somewhat more than six, but the most imaginative of all, perhaps, was the fable that Roosevelt rarely if ever saw the "Magic" intercept transcripts, despite being first on the list of intended recipients via the joint Army-Navy delivery system. This has been advanced with the airy and casual aplomb of someone reporting that it is raining outside. When placed against the many-times-told account of the delivery to the President of the "Magic" intercept of the first thirteen parts

---

[‡] (Neumann, "World War I Revisionist," in Arthur Goddard, ed., *Harry Elmer Barnes, Learned Crusader: The New History in Action* [Colorado Springs: Ralph Myles, Publisher, 1968], p. 261.)

of the Japanese Memorandum #902 shortly after 9 p.m. the evening of Dec. 6, and his agitated response upon reading it, surely it must stretch the credulity of even his most devoted self-serving partisans to the cracking point to be told this was one of his rare exposures to these English language transcripts of intercepted Japanese diplomatic intelligence traffic. Several historians of England and the British Empire have declared that the Russians in their campaigns against Napoleon conducted their intelligence service in the language of the enemy, French. This "Magic" windfall surely was the next best thing to that, and one can hardly expect the American Chief of State to be ignorant of it in the manner described by his apologists.

[2] David Brown and W. Richard Bruner, eds., *I Can Tell It Now,* by members of the Overseas Press Club. Foreword by Dwight D. Eisenhower, 363 pp. New York: Dutton, 1964.

[3] The Defense Department, instead of publishing the "Magic" intercepts in chronological order, or all of the traffic between any two points (e.g., Panama-Tokyo or Tokyo-Bangkok) all in one place, has arranged them in various sequences, some of which are a little fanciful or imaginative, but probably making more sense to those with mainly technical interest in the content. But one effect of this procedure, or "methodology," if one prefers contemporary cliches, is in effect the preparation of a scheme leading to a sort of history of the 15 months before Pearl by themselves, unintentional or otherwise.

Scattered through this assemblage of what is supposed to be exclusively "Magic" derived from translated intercepts of Japanese intelligence are several pieces of American Naval communications which are not part of "Magic" at all, and seem to be inserted at strategic spots which convey the impression of being self-serving additions to the potential account which might result from using this material. Some of this may also have the intention of reinforcing the official line on innocence of Pearl Harbor being the primary attack point for the Japanese upon rupture of diplomatic relations.

However, there is one especially interesting dispatch included *("Magic" Background,* Vol. IV Appendix, pp. A-109/A-110) from the Chief of Naval Operations (Adm. Stark) to the Commander-in-Chief of the U.S. Far Eastern Fleet (Adm. Thomas C. Hart) (#271442, Nov. 26, 1941, the same date as that of the State Department's "ultimatum" to Japan). This instructs Adm. Hart to wage, at the outset of a state of belligerency with Japan, *unrestricted* submarine and aerial warfare south and west of an area bounded by 7° and 30° North Latitude and 122° and 140° East Longitude. The region covered by these stipulated compass points incorporates the Philippines and the Philippine Sea, and some areas of British and Dutch interest as well, and was to be treated as a "strategic area." The unrestricted warfare was to be conducted south and west of this, presumably in the areas of the South China Sea, plus the environs of Singapore, Malaya in general, the Dutch East Indies and the region stretching into and including the Gulf of Siam (Thailand) and adjacent areas of the seacoast of the French Indo-Chinese colonies, now Vietnam, Laos, and Cambodia (Kampuchea).

Adm. Hart was further instructed to work in liaison with the British and Dutch forces in defining the circumstances under which this vast region of the Far Eastern waters was to be policed, but it was especially interesting that Adm. Stark specifically cautioned Adm. Hart that in dealing with the leaders of these two other powers he was to "take care not to disclose for the present these instructions to wage unrestricted submarine and aerial warfare."

This communication said nothing about Army cooperation or any contingency priority deriving from the Army until two days later, when Adm. Stark's # 271912CR0863 informed Adm. Hart that Gen. Marshall had requested that Gen. MacArthur be informed so that the Army Air Force might "make appropriate plans" to cooperate with this unrestricted warfare plan. (This writer has repeatedly encountered in recent years individuals who reflect a faint smile and murmur, upon hearing such details of 40 years ago, "I didn't know the Army has its own air force," and must conclude that he is in the presence of someone who does not go back very far.)

We thus have additional information about American plans for southeast Asia, and further confirmation that a concerted effort to wage offensive war versus Japan was substantially envisioned well before the Hawaiian attack, as opposed to the general misconception of mindless lazing-about in huddled defensiveness a la *From Here to Eternity* in utter ignorance of the Pacific realities.

That this contingency involved deception of "allies" as to the decision to wage unrestricted submarine and aerial war in a large area of the East Asian waters is of more than casual importance, and suggests that such a change had been made by the Administration and the Joint Chiefs of Staff as a secret decision to "revise" the arrangements previously incorporated in the Rainbow/ WPL-46 understanding arrived at during the extended meetings in Singapore between January 29th and March 27th, 1941. That the Japanese had rather quickly found out about these meetings, where Rainbow had been born, has been suggested by a variety of reactions, but whether they found out about Adm. Stark's Nov. 26 message to Adm. Hart is uncertain. Constant interest in Tokyo concerning the presence and movement of U.S. submarines in Manila, in addition to news about troop movements in the Philippines and the disposition of Army fighting aircraft, accelerated in November, 1941 but in part preceded Adm. Stark's 'unrestricted warfare' pronouncement. Submarines far outnumbered other U.S. Navy craft based in Manila and vicinity, and two "Purple" messages from there to Tokyo Nov. 24 and Nov. 26, intercepted by American intelligence and available for consultation in English translation a short time later, mentioned some two dozen U.S. submarines leaving Manila Bay, "destination unknown." On the general interest in submarine movement one can consult the following Japanese "Purple" dispatches: #742 (Nov. 8, 1941); #745 (Nov. 10, 1941); #757 (Nov. 14, 1941); #767 (Nov. 15, 1941); #785 (Nov. 22, 1941); #790 (Nov. 25, 1941); #805 (Nov. 29, 1941); #812 (Dec. 1, 1941). The last two were not translated until Dec. 8 according to official records but the others were available as "Magic" intercepts shortly after each of the original sending dates in question. The messages mentioned above have been reproduced in *The "Magic" Background Of Pearl Harbor,* Vol. IV Appendix, pp. A-161/A-170.

In retrospect, this U.S. plan for the conducting of unrestricted submarine warfare was resolutely put into operation after Dec. 7, 1941. In a shrewd and percipient commentary on the U.S. Senate ratification of the four Geneva Conventions of August 12, 1949 by a vote of 77-0 in July, 1955, summarizing their essential futility and predicting their sure coming violation by future belligerents (so amply vindicated by what happened between 1955 and 1980), the *Chicago Tribune* ("Civilizing War," July 11, 1955) pointed out the grave Allied violation during World War II of the previous protocols of this sort, especially the Hague Convention of 1907, the Washington conference of 1922, the Geneva Convention of 1928 and the London naval treaty of 1930. As to the latter the *Tribune* pointed out pithily,

. . . the laws governing submarine warfare were clearly and precisely defined in the London naval treaty of 1930, which specified that attacks were to be confined to unmistakable men o' war, and then only after seeing to the safety of all hands. The American navy, in its official report on the submarine campaign against Japan, admitted an indiscriminate campaign in which nine of every 10 Japanese ships sunk were noncombatant vessels. Of 276,000 Japanese drowned in these attacks, 105,000 were civilians.

Among the rarest of all the narratives of history is an account of the indictment, successful prosecution and punishment of the *winners* of a war for violations of international law governing the conduct of belligerency. In the round of post-World War II trials in Germany conducted by the U.S. under Allied Control Council Law No. 10, when German defense counsel pointed out Allied breaches of the Hague Conventions of 1899 and 1907 during the war, spokesmen among the prosecutors such as Telford Taylor airily dismissed the pertinent articles of these Conventions as inapplicable to Allied behavior because they were "antiquarian." Some wry comments on such selective application of international law can be found in such books as those by August von Knieriem, *The Nuremberg Trials* (Chicago: Regnery, 1959) and Werner Maser, *Nurnberg: Tribunal der Sieger* (Dusseldorf: Econ Verlag, 1977), rendered in fanciful English translation as *Nuremberg: A Nation on Trial* (New York: Charles Scribner's Sons, 1979).

[4]Grew's report to the State Department is undoubtedly the best-known and most widely divulged pseudo-intelligence tidbit allowed to reach the American public. This may have been an electrifying possibility to Sec. of State Hull, but could hardly have stirred much response from the Navy, which had already rehearsed two Pearl Harbor attacks on their own in simulated war games off Hawaii in the half dozen or so years prior to the outbreak of war in Europe in September, 1939. Probably picked up third hand as a consequence of drunken talk at a diplomatic cocktail party, there is an almost-comic dwelling upon its significance in the book *The Pearl Harbor Cover-Up* by Frank Schuler and Robin Moore (New York: Pinnacle Books, 1976). In parts this book reads like a brief in behalf of the pro-Maoist wing in the State Department's version of how war came in the Pacific.

What is missing from the record, to the release of the "Magic" intercepts by the Defense Department just recently, is the simultaneous war scare in the Japanese Foreign Office, a matter of even greater curiosity. On February 15, 1941 the Japanese vice-consul in Honolulu, Otohiro Okuda, dispatched his #027, which was addressed to the Foreign Ministry for routing to the General Staff and the chief of Japanese Naval Intelligence, American Section, Capt. Kenji Ogawa. This relayed second hand information that the

Roosevelt Administration would declare war on Japan sometime between the sending date and the end of the first week of March.

Since American intelligence had cracked "Purple" almost six months previous to this, it may be that Japanese intelligence in Hawaii had been victimized by the process we now call "dis-information," in an effort to determine how long it would take to be released in Japan, being able to read both transmission and return reaction with equal ease. Nothing has been made public via release of appropriate "Magic" intercepts as to how this sensational piece of non-fact was handled or whether any response was made to this manufactured war scare. In view of the mollifying press conference given by Japan's new ambassador to the U.S.A., Adm. Kichisaburo Nomura, on Feb. 20 (he had just arrived in Washington on Feb. 11), the Japanese Foreign Office seems not to have taken seriously this prediction of a war declaration by the U.S.A. Nevertheless both Japan and the U.S.A. on the highest diplomatic levels went through separate war scares in the first two months of 1941.

Whether both were the result of deliberate incitement by one another's "dis-information" agents can only be ruminated upon at this point. But there is no doubt of Japanese interest in possible U.S. Navy action in the event of a state of war during this time, as the intercepts #011 and #029 (neither of which are in the Defense Department's published collection of "Magic") attest. As one can see, these reports on ship-harbor activities in Pearl Harbor began well before the presence in Honolulu of the new Japanese consul general, Nagao Kita, who first arrived on March 14, 1941. (Though Kita's name is associated with similar reports to Japan dealing with what was going on in Pearl Harbor starting in September, it is obvious that this latter was well after a stream of "Purple" intercepts indicated that in the event of trouble between the two countries, Hawaii was a prime target for an early if not initiating attack by Japanese forces. Even Farago, in his essentially establishment-supporting book *The Broken Seal,* concedes as much. Though American intelligence never found in their interceptions of traffic of the Japanese Imperial Navy one word even hinting that Pearl Harbor might be a future target, Farago concedes, "On the other hand, 'Magic' produced this evidence actually in abundance, from February 15, 1941, until the morning of the attack.") *(The Broken Seal,* p. 167.)

[5] Some idea of the richness of the obscurantism and diversionary genius now applied to the Pearl Harbor epic as we approach

the 40th anniversary of the attack can be derived especially from fairly current histories of wartime intelligence. Especially revealing is how the subject is handled in William R. Carson's *The Armies of Ignorance: The Rise of the American Intelligence Empire* (New York: Dial/James Wade, 1977, pp. 151-159). After a brief treatment excoriating those who reject the official establishment line as "isolationists" enamored of "conspiratorial" fixations, Carson manages to sketch out the layers of camouflage which have been laid upon the subject over the years, while getting to mention only two students of the affair, the undeviating establishment apologists and chroniclers, Mrs. Wohlstetter and Hans L. Trefousse. No one is to blame, and the author seems to believe that the main trouble was that not enough people were privy to the "Magic" intercepts to enable the dispatch of a proper "warning" to the Hawaii commanders. That every responsible figure in the highest authority echelons was quite conversant with or on the automatic delivery list for "Magic," including the President, his Secretaries of State, War, and Navy, the Chief of Staff and the Chief of Naval Operations, and the very top commanders in the intelligence departments of the armed services, does not appear to impress or to have been adequate according to Carson. How an underling with less knowledge could have gone over the heads of this group of men to "warn" Pearl Harbor escapes all understanding. But the unknown ignorant and unauthorized all appear to gain in stature and importance in the wake of the event, when anything they might have attempted to say or do would have left them vulnerable to swift censure and possible demotion, in addition to offhand dismissal of their words or actions.

Further evidence that histories of intelligence in harmony with accepted official positions prefer to come no closer than the views of 20 years ago, and conclude in a consensus that Mrs. Wohlstetter had the last word in 1962, can be found in Ronald Lewin's *Ultra Goes to War* (New York: McGraw-Hill, 1978). "Ultra" (as the British named it) was the German analog of the Japanese "Purple" code, and the actual "Magic" intercepts circulated by American intelligence all bore the word "Ultra" rubber-stamped on them. Lewin's view is close to Carson's, but is more subdued, though similarly following closely in support of the too-mixed-"signals," no-one-could-be-blamed obscurantism of Mrs. Wohlstetter's *Pearl Harbor: Warning and Decision*. The position taken by Lewin not only requires ignoring the multitude of errors in this latter book, in part pointed out by Percy Greaves and Charles C. Hiles, but also a most selective approach to the matter of the chain of command, approvingly pinpointed when something of credit is to be assigned, but studiously avoided when something blameworthy demands the designation of some responsibility.

[6] An unusual development in this dramatic account relating to the significance of the Briggs interview, unprecedented in the literature related to the Pearl Harbor topic, was the publication of the entire interview, from a facsimile copy originally deposited in the National Archives, in the Fall, 1980 (No. 24) *Newsletter* of the American Committee on the History of the Second World War, a solidly official-establishment organization, with presumably no real interest in this kind of disclosure. The reproduction indicates the elisions and other deletions made in the copy made available to other scholars previously (the *Newsletter* did not make its appearance until around Christmas time, 1980 despite its date), and which substantial interest from March, 1980 onward on the part of several investigators undoubtedly precipitated. But the persistence of deleted material even forty years after the event helps to convey the impression that we are still too close to the event to allow full disclosure.

There is a mysterious aspect of the Briggs Winds Execute matter which requires some official explanation and extended discourse. Though the previous accounts for 35 years have centered on Captain Safford's repeated insistence on its receipt December 4, the material related to the Briggs interview recently made public clearly indicates the latter originally received the Winds message *December 2,* which actually makes the official gloss on the matter look even worse.